S0-BWL-720

EVOLUTION AND THE SIN IN EDEN

A New Christian Synthesis

Anthony Zimmerman, STD

University Press of America,® Inc.
Lanham • New York • Oxford

WITHDRAWN
HIEBERT LIBRARY
FRESNO PACIFIC UNIV.-M. B. SEMINARY
FRESNO, CA 93702

Copyright © 1998
University Press of America,® Inc.
4720 Boston Way
Lanham, Maryland 20706

12 Hid's Copse Rd.
Cumnor Hill, Oxford OX2 9JJ

All rights reserved
Printed in the United States of America
British Library Cataloging in Publication Information Available

Library of Congress Cataloging-in-Publication Data

Zimmerman, Anthony.
Evolution and the sin of Eden : a new Christian synthesis / Anthony
Zimmerman.
p.   cm.
Includes bibliographical references and index.
l. Creation. 2. Sin. 3. Speech. 4. Catholic Church—Doctrines.
I. Title.
BL226.Z54 1998   233'.1—dc21   98-42202 CIP

ISBN 0-7618-1277-6 (cloth: alk. ppr.)

⊖™ The paper used in this publication meets the minimum
requirements of American National Standard for Information
Sciences—Permanence of Paper for Printed Library Materials,
ANSI Z39.48—1984

CONTENTS

FOREWORD

We shoot ourselves in the foot if we believe, as many do, that Adam did harm to our natural selves. His sin deprives us of grace at birth, but Christ restores that with Baptism, and provides generous bonuses besides. God does not strike our natures with lightning because of original sin.

Adam is not our enemy in the spiritual combat. It is our sound and rambunctious natural selves which prefer to remain grooved into things of this world rather than be prodded up the stairs into heaven by demands of grace. We are needlessly pessimistic about our "fallen" condition.

Pope St. Leo the Great assessed the sin in Eden as a net gain, not a disaster. In Sermon 2 *De Res.* he enthused:

> Happy, had he not fallen from how God made him;
> Happier, if he manages to remain as God re-made him.
> *Felix, si ab eo non decideret, quod Deus fecit;*
> *Felicior, si in eo maneret, quod refecit.*

Golden-tongued St. John Chrysostom tells us why: "We have not merely received a medicine that is capable of healing our wounds, but in addition health, beauty, honor, glory, and dignities that vastly surpass our natural condition" (Sermon 10, Letter to Romans; see Scheeben 420).

In this book science frequently interfaces with faith. Both can grow thereby. St. Augustine boasted that faith sheds light on the natural sciences: "Understanding is the reward of faith." he said. May this be your reward as you read on.

I hereby express thanks and appreciation to all whose words I cite and quote, which I carefully annotate.
Anthony Zimmerman, Nagoya, Japan, June 13, 1998.

Chapter 1

SPEECH AND REVELATION

If we ask whether our first human ancestors had a mature sense of responsibility, of right and wrong, a knowledge about duties toward God and toward each other, the answer can be no other than yes. God would not have held them responsible for disobedience if they had lacked a fully adult sense of duty. The Bible indicates that the Lord God treated our Adam and Eve as adults when He called them to an accounting for their flagrant disobedience, heard their excuses and confessions, gave them their penance, and then restored the previous relationship of friendly intimacy with them on new terms after they had learned from their experience.

The story of original sin, as related in the Bible and as taught in the Catechism, implies that our Adam and Eve were not half-illumined creatures barely emerged from an animal world, but that they were fully human. They were speaking with God and with each other in an intelligible language about serious problems of life and existence. God revealed Himself to them, and we know that He does not speak into a vacuum. They understood what He said.

This fact in turn provides us with the vital information which is absolutely essential for reasonable discussion about human evolution, namely that our first ancestors spoke an intelligible language. They possessed the capacity to arrange in their minds the ideas which God had revealed. They understood the do's and don'ts of His revelation and what He expected of them, and could discuss these matters with each other and with their children.

That our primeval ancestors were monogamists is another indication of their normal and adult sense of responsibility. Their monogamous status is recorded in Genesis, and is a revelation which Christ confirmed when He responded to an interrogation by the Pharisees about divorce. Christ's response contrasts the more lax behavior of the Israelites with the strict conformity to lifetime fidelity of our first ancestors:

> Have you not read that he who made them from the beginning made them male and female, and said "For this reason a man shall leave his father and mother and be joined to his wife, and the two shall become one"? (Mt 19:4-5). [*The Revised Standard Version* is used unless indicated otherwise.]

By so re-constituting mandatory monogamy with this reference to behavior at "the beginning," Christ identified our primeval ancestors as members of our race, as responsible persons, who married, who remained faithful, who educated their children. Our family tree dates back to them. Christ bade us to do as they had done. He thereby manifested His esteem for our first parents.

As an aside, I feel sorry that the Church doesn't celebrate our Adam and Eve with liturgical honors now at the turn of the millennia. In all the careful preparations made by the Vatican for the events of the year 2000, I read not one word of praise and respect for our honorable first ancestors. Such an omission is not in sync with Christ who upheld the first couple as the original model of marital fidelity. It is not in sync with the Bible in which Sirach extols Adam as Number One in the human race: "Adam above every living being in the creation" (Sir 49:16). No family ever celebrates an anniversary without inviting the grandparents. The Church formerly commemorated Adam and Eve on December 24, the day before Christmas. And yet when preparing to celebrate the year 2000 the Vatican is apparently forgetting about our debt of gratitude to our first parents. Why? I don't know why. How sad, I say. The first parents of the human race certainly merit a word of thanks and congratulations from us at this turn of the century and millennium. Now back to our theme.

SPEECH ORGANS IN THE FOSSIL RECORD

Modern speech organs - the larynx, pharynx and accompanying structures which we use in daily speaking - are anchored to a specific type of bone structure - specific to Homo Sapiens. That structure does not appear in the fossil record of the human line until several hundred thousand years ago. It delineates a time-framework within which scientists can theorize about the period in which humans became capable of speaking with the very rapid flow of words characteristic of modern languages. For us it very conveniently also provides a date - albeit not very precise - when our first ancestors lived, and therefore when they committed original sin.

The truth that the persons who first committed original sin possessed an adult sense of responsibility implies that they arranged their thoughts in linguistic patterns. For without modern language ability, they would be extremely handicapped from thinking logically enough to be held responsible by God for committing original sin.

LANGUAGE INDICATES AN IMMATERIAL SOUL

Human speech displays the existence of a mind, of a person whose being transcends atomic and molecular bricks of matter. Our ability to speak marks us off very distinctly as differing from animals. We speak, we think, but they do neither. Between us and them yawns an enormous metaphysical space whose expanses no animal can cross. If our human bodies evolved and graduated from animal life -- there are good reasons to believe so -- our spiritual souls did not sprout from animal seed. Animals feel but they do not think; nor can their lives generate thinking souls. Moreover, even humans do not provide souls for their children:

> The Church teaches that every spiritual soul is created immediately by God - it is not "produced" by the parents - and also that it is immortal; it does not perish when it separates from the body at death, and it will be reunited with the body at the final Resurrection (*The Catechism of the Catholic Church* 366, hereinafter referenced as *CCC*).

We can teach some animals to reproduce a limited repertoire of sounds which resemble speech. Prized parakeets can greet us with a friendly crackle of a practiced "Good morning!" But try as we might, we can't teach parakeets or any other living creature to discourse logically with us in speech. The very nature of logical thought is spiritual, and animals show no sign of spiritual equipment to think with. They build nests, they greet the dawn with song, they nuzzle and they pair off, but they don't make binding contracts, they don't recognize right from wrong, and they don't ever bring litigation to courts of law.

Humans, on the contrary, luxuriate in the joys of reasoning and thinking, of matching cause and effect, of living in a constant awareness of what is right and what is wrong, of neighborly gossip and discourse about national scandals, of declaiming with pretentious political rhetoric and sonorous decibels about justice, peace and order, of making intelligible choice in favor of what is good and beautiful and splendid, of looking beyond this temporal life on earth to an even better life in the mysterious realm of heaven. Animals know nothing about life in the hereafter. Nothing. Speech is one immovable boundary marker set between humans and animals.

We assume appropriately that our Adam and Eve knew right from wrong, for otherwise God would not have held them responsible. Pushing the logic one step further, we assume that they were a people capable of speaking a human language. Humans don't understand responsibilities unless they can resonate them on linguistic sounding boards. Those to whom God spoke His primeval revelation must have been able to understand His spoken word, to interiorize in their minds the concepts He communicated, to then fix the concepts on coded sounds wherewith they were able to discourse about the message with spouse and children. To do this the couple whom the Bible locates in the Garden in Eden must have had advanced linguistic ability, comparable to speech competence of adults today. They were not mere children whose thoughts and language were rudimentary, nor were they dizzied adolescents recently emerged from an ape population but not yet able to cope with adult human problems.

THOUGHT ANCHORS ITSELF ON SPEECH

It is an observable fact that whenever we think we instinctively, and of necessity, speak these thoughts, whether
inwardly or outwardly. Intellectual activity is, of course, a
spiritual reality, and we may be convinced that we think
without speech. Often we are hardly aware that we project
our thoughts on a perceptible screen of phonetic symbols
and syntactic arrangements as a habit, practically by
necessity. But if we watch ourselves closely, we can
observe that whenever we think, we anchor the thoughts
into speech patterns.

On the other hand it must be said that we somehow also
do our thinking without complete dependence on words,
phrases, and sentences. For we appear to think first, then
fish for words to express and anchor the thought. Also,
when we translate from one language to another, we
extract the thought from the original language and hold it
in suspense while we fish with this thought for an appropriate word. To think, then, is a process which our immaterial
soul initiates, but this spirit immediately calls upon linguistic
crutches for support.

Thought is a fleeting reality which differs from speech, but
it does not fly high nor long unless it supports itself on
wings of language. Deliberation somehow exists immaterial-
ly but unfolds itself upon material images. Opinion and
judgment appear to be independent even of the brain. We
use the brain as an artist uses his violin to resonate the
music he has in mind. With the brain as an instrument we
pattern into sentences our prefabricated or emerging
thought. We stimulate the brain to produce linguistic
resonance to shape and clarify and solidify the thought we

have in mind. Then finally we use the brain to orchestrate the ensemble of speech organs to display our thoughts externally. We encode our thoughts upon audio or visual symbols which others can decode to obtain insight into the thoughts we are belaboring.

We need words and language to think with speed, clarity, and logic. Even while you are reading this, your thoughts latch onto the written words to anchor themselves. They may race ahead of what you read, and you may check back to get back on track. The point is, we are always seeking to rest our thoughts upon linguistic patterns. At any rate, to anchor, to shape, and to sharpen our spiritual thoughts, we constantly project them upon sensually perceptible images -- on sounds, sights, touches, tastes, scents, and movements -- but always and primarily, on linguistic patterns.

When we think without audible speaking, we nevertheless pour out a constant stream of sensory images, mostly linguistic and in our mother tongue, upon which we sustain, shape, untangle, sharpen, and finally understand our thoughts clearly. Day or night, while awake, we do a running commentary in our own mind about our selves, about the world around us, about our actions. We use words, words, and more words while doing so, sometimes arranged in syntactical order, sometimes in snatches of incomplete phrases. We speak, and we listen to our own speech.

The mind attends, it observes, it compares, it remembers, it ponders, it meditates, it day-dreams, and it sifts evidence, it draws conclusions, it develops a theme, and it solves a problem. In other words, it thinks, in the narrow sense of the term. Can this go on without words? ... One thing is certain: thought is not happy working in the void - even if it can work there at all. It has a fondness for sense material. It seems to need something with which to steady itself and maintain its grip on real experience. So it seeks an anchorage in percepts and images...If thought can proceed without language it cannot proceed very far. For long sustained trains of thought language is absolutely necessary (P.H. Ballard, *Thought and Language*, p. 30;40).

We lose our ability to think when our physical brain is hindered from resonating our thoughts on words and other images, as when we are knocked unconscious or otherwise inhibited. The thinking we perhaps do without sensory images is beyond the boundary of our conscious awareness. We become aware only when we grasp hold of the thought with sense images; with images of sound, sight, movement, touch, smell, or a combination of sense images, almost always arranged into a language pattern.

GOD REVEALED HIMSELF TO AN ADAM AND EVE WHO SPOKE A LANGUAGE

In the year 1546 the Council of Trent articulated in precise theological canons the nature of certain gifts which God gave to our first ancestors. In addition to their natural endowments, God enriched them by modifying their spirits with an addition of supernatural capacities. Trent termed the enrichment "holiness and justice,"(*Denzinger-Schoenmetzer, Enchiridion Symbolorum, ed. 34*, No.1511, hereinafter indicated by *DS*). The gift they received was a supernatural endowment, a modification into a higher dimension of being, an infusion of superior and heavenly light and strength into their natural powers of knowledge and volition, such as we also receive at the time of Baptism. The bestowal of this supernatural gift implies that God also revealed Himself to our first parents. God would not enrich them with the gift, and hold them responsible for subsequent action to act in accordance with the gift, without also providing them by way of revelation with all the instructions they needed to conduct themselves properly as newly adopted children of God.

The belief that God "manifested Himself to our first parents from the very beginning" (*CCC* 54) leads to wide-ranging conclusions concerning their linguistic ability. We reason that they comprehended God's revelation in linguistic patterns, whose meaning they understood, whose contents they could articulate, whose connotation they would teach to their children. Vatican II affirmed that God "wishing to open up the way of heavenly salvation, manifested himself to our first parents from the very beginning. After the fall, he buoyed them up with the hope of salvation, by promising redemption" (*Dei Verbum* 3; see also *CCC* 375;376). The significant conclusion follows that our Adam and Eve were not primitives with still undeveloped minds, but were adults who could think no less ably than we do. The vehicle for receiving the revelation and for communicating it to others was the language of human speech.

The contents of the primeval revelation must have included basic matters which the human mind could already know in some manner but not yet with the gemlike clarity and cut precision of the same truths newly understood after God had emblazoned them upon their minds through divine revelation. The primeval communication illumined with light as of the noonday sun the truths that God exists, that He alone made heaven and earth and controls all things, that He had also created them and united them in monogamous marriage.

What was special in God's encounter with our first ancestors was an additional revelation that no human mind could ever guess or know without a revelation; namely that God "destined us in love to be his sons...according to the purpose of his will, to the praise of his glorious grace which he freely bestowed on us" (Eph 1:5-6). It is the mystery that God is pleased to adopt humans into the divine family by means of grace, with the intention of admiting them into God's eternal presence with the beatific vision in life after death. After revealing this to our first parents, we reason that He also taught them a code of behavior suitable for God's royal family. It would be essentially the same Ten Commandments which He also revealed to Moses.

We correctly reason that Adam and Eve must have taught their children that the Lord is their God and they must adore Him alone. They must reverence Him and keep holy His name. They shall pray to Him at regular times (but probably there was no Sabbath in the first revelation). Children are to honor and obey father and mother. Adults must not murder, must not be unfaithful to their monogamous marriage partner, must not steal, lie, nor be envious. In brief, they were enjoined to live as royalty does, to conduct themselves with noble behavior as befits membership in the divine family. Their brief life on earth was to be a time of testing, of combat under challenge, of growth in authentic obedience to the Creator God.

REVELATION TRANSMITTED BY LANGUAGE

As we shall develop more fully in subsequent chapters, modern speech facility was lacking to all manner of people who lived before or even contemporaneously with Homo Sapiens. Scientists such as Philip Lieberman who research the fossil record, incomplete though it be, believe that the Neanderthals, Homo Erectus, and Homo Habilis were unable to master a language with rapid-firing speech as we do. Our modern speech organs would not have fit into their skeletal framework. Lieberman believes that it was Homo Sapiens who could first speak a modern language, at most perhaps 400,000 to 250,000 years ago (see *The Biology and Evolution of Language* (1984) pp. 306-316).

We take it from there to argue that if the speech ability of people living before Homo Sapiens appeared was rudimentary, their thinking powers were not yet developed sufficiently to function as adults who could commit original sin. God would not hold immature humans responsible for original sin, which was a mortal sin. Homo Sapiens of quite recent times is the only type of human who could qualify linguistically for life in the Garden of Eden -- that is, for the kind of adult thinking and speaking which our faith necessarily associates with our first parents whom God held responsible for original sin. They must have been able to speak so rapidly that logical discourse of some complexity could be compacted into meaningful words and syntax before the logical ensemble would fall out of the short term memory. Such is the thrust of the argumentation in this chapter.

Chapter 2

MARVELS OF HUMAN SPEECH

Specialists who have researched fossils of the Neander-thals, Homo Erectus and Homo Habilis conclude that these early people could not have spoken a human language as fluently and as richly articulated as we are able to do. Our advanced type of speech organs would not have fit into their skeletal forms. Logic compels us, however, to reason that the people who committed original sin, who had received revelation from God and were aware of their responsibilities, were endowed with advanced linguistic abilities. This chapter treats about the marvels of human speech, aiming to acquaint ourselves more fully with the abilities of the ancestors who committed original sin.

We speak daily with such ease that we pay little attention to the myriad mechanisms which go into its production. "The motor control patterns that are necessary for pro-duction of human speech are probably the most complex maneuvers that a human being can produce," writes Lieberman ("On the Evolution of Human Syntactic Ability," *Journal of Human Evolution* (1985), p. 659). Somehow we manage to articulate what we are thinking and feeling by means of audible signals which are deciphered meaningfully by the hearer. When we engage in conversation our brains, speech organs, eyes, ears, faces, and our entire bodies get into the act. The 13 billion nerves of the brain become engaged and swing into action, or stand by for service if needed. Both the speaker and the listener keep track of the nuanced words and sentences in their short-term memories and anchor their thoughts on them, or deduce meaning from them.

The meaning of a sentence is usually not known until we hear the end of it. With the short-term memory to hold the entire sentence momentarily in view, we typically scramble the sequential verbiage into an emulsified porridge, swirling together the subject, the predicate, the object, together with modifiers. Only then, with the entire sentence in a bird's eye view, do we grasp its meaning. We mix into the emulsified concept the flavor of whatever emotions may have been expressed in the speech production, love, anger, contempt, admiration, whatever.

When the passage of time that has gone into the production of a sentence exceeds the time limitations of our short term memory, however, we have difficulties. By the time the end of sentence which is too long for the short term memory is reached, the beginning of that discourse may have fallen out of the short term memory. When the short-term memory cannot present to the mind an entire sentence, its beginning, its end, and all that is in between, so that the mind can work on it as one piece, we lose sight of its meaning. We hear or see words, but cannot perceive a projected picture of their meaning. If we speak a complex and long sentence too slowly, therefore, our listener may not comprehend what we are trying to say. To communicate highly developed concepts intelligibly, we need to produce speech in rapid fire sequence, with clearly articulated phonemes, and preferably with a well nuanced mode and flow of expression.

Lieberman and other scientists theorize that speech production by Habilis, Erectus, and Neanderthal must have been slow and elementary in comparison with ours. Handicapped in this manner, they could not have compressed complicated meanings into the short-term memory for what we consider to be standard intellectual communication. Their sentences were presumably short and simple, and enunciated at perhaps one tenth of the speed at which we ordinarily speak. The range of articulation was also less developed than our rich thesaurus of well articulated phonemes. If that is true, then we can reason that the abstract concepts associated with the revelation given to our Adam and Eve would have been beyond the powers of comprehension as well as of communication for hominids other than Homo Sapiens. Presumably these other hominids lacked not only our very highly developed speech organs; the neurological substratum was deficient as well. Lieberman bases this conclusion on the fact that our organs would simply not have fit into the framework of the basicranium and the connecting vertebrae of hominids other than Homo Sapiens.

We take it from there to theorize that if their ability to speak was thus underdeveloped, their powers of thinking would be similarly limited. The people who committed original sin, who could understand God's revelation and teach it to their children, indicated by their action that they could speak and think much as adults of today. Therefore we can conclude that our Adam and Eve were not Homo Habilis types of people who lived up to two and a half million years ago, nor were they ancient Homo Erectus or Neanderthals. The speech of these predecessors of Homo Sapiens was too limited in scope to cope with the events narrated in Genesis. God would not have held such people responsible for the commission of original sin if they were unable to speak and think with adult capabilities.

Our basis for this reasoning is what scientists deduce from the evidence found in the fossil record. Lieberman reasons that Neanderthals, Erectus, and Habilis spoke with far less sophistication than we do, and at a speed of perhaps only one tenth of our fluent flow of words:

> The presence of a fully encoded speech system in recent hominids may also have more directly contributed to the development of complex syntactic organization in human languages. The rapid data rate of human speech allows us to transmit a long sequence of words within a short interval. We can take the words that constitute a complex sentence into short-term memory and can effect a syntactic and semantic analysis. We have to keep track of the group of words that constitute a sentence in order to comprehend its meaning. Deficits like dyslexia, which interfere with a reader's ability to take in strings of words in a short time, thus often result in syntactic deficits. Dyslexic readers have difficulty in decoding the complex syntactic structures that occur in written material because they read words so slowly that they forget the words that started the sentence before they can analyze the sentence.

Because it took so much time for them to produce the words of their already limited vocabulary, continues Lieberman, they would have been unable to concatenate complex sentences:

> The effects of a characteristically low rate of speech communication throughout the entire hominid population thus would probably limit syntactic complexity. Given the same constraints on short-term memory that are evident in modern

Homo sapiens, a speech rate that was one-tenth of modern speech would limit vocal communication to very simple syntactic structures (Lieberman 1984, 325).

He suggests, in this context, that we make an experiment: that we read a long sentence at one-tenth of the speed of the normal reading rate. By the time we reach the end of such a slowly read sentence, we forget what its beginning was, and so we lose track of its meaning. Further interaction or repetition then becomes necessary.

Lieberman measured the basi-cranium of various hominids, including Neanderthal, and found that our speech organs would not fit into their framework:

The long palates of Australopithecine, *homo erectus*, and classic Neanderthal fossils instead must support nonhuman standard-plan supralaryngeal vocal tracts, in which the tongue is long and thin and is positioned almost entirely within the oral cavity" (Lieberman 1984, 296).

Consequently these non-Homo Sapiens hominids were unable to pronounce distinctly our vowels of [a] and [i] and [u], and the [k] and [g] stops which are essential for rapid speech calibration (Lieberman 1984, 318).

The three vowel sounds mentioned above are produced when we format our speaking tubes to produce and resonate the vowel sound within them. We do this instinctively, with the help of the automatisms we have partially inherited and partially developed through practice. The formatting of the speaking tubes may be compared to sliding the tubes of a trombone up and down, or pressing the keys of trumpet and flute to resonate the desired pitch. Or, we might think of a pipe organ with many pipes of different size and configuration, each measured to resonate a pitch at its calibrated frequency with total response. Our speaking tubes shape themselves continually into changed forms, which might be compared with hundreds of pipe organ units. We change the "speech pipes" swiftly and constantly to formulate and resonate our words. The tubes are in constant motion to re-adjust themselves to resonate the desired sound and to give it additional articulation.

Our clever Homo Sapiens speech tubes can shape themselves almost instantly to resonate the designated vowel sounds as we desire, and with a smoothness and efficiency which leaves us unaware of the masterful performances. Our air tube, being in a vertical position as it leaves the lungs, proceeds through the larynx (Adam's apple) and upwards; then it makes a sharp turn to the horizontal when issued through the mouth. We call it a two-tube system, with modifications of formatting taking place in the vertical section as one tube, and in the horizontal section as the second tube, with a sharp turn between which is also adjustable like a valve. This is in contrast to the single tube system of animals as well as of non-Homo Sapiens hominids. Their single tube routes the flow of air in a comparatively straight passage from lung to mouth and nose, without making that sharp turn from vertical to horizontal, without a possibility of different resonances in two tubes, and sophisticated modification maneuvers within them and in the connecting valve.

The two tube system of Home Sapiens capacitates us to format and articulate an immense repertoire of phonemes and to produce them in rapid succession. The pharynx and the oral cavity, segmented at the turn, enable us to be extremely versatile in producing speech. The tongue of Homo Sapiens, its vertical section in the throat, its adaptable muscle in the mouth, is specifically capacitated to format the different sections for vowels. To produce an [a] (AAAH) vowel sound, we format the mouth into a spacious hollow tube to boom the vowel while we compress the vertical tube into a pressurized constricted narrow passage. To produce an [i] (EEEE) vowel, we command the tongue to do just the opposite, to open wide the vertical and constrict the horizontal to compress outward this high pitch vowel. To produce a [u] (MOOO) we constrict the gateway between the vertical and horizontal tubes, sounding the vowel with both tubes open.

How our spiritual free will gives the commands for the two tubes to format themselves in relation to each other in order to resonate the desired sounds remains a mystery. Animals do this by instinct. We likewise perform speech of a far more sophisticated and complex nature by way of instinct and acquired automatisms. But we remain aware of being in control of our speech actions so that we speak as intellect and will decide. This is one of the great mysteries of life, namely how immaterial commands of the soul operate the material instruments of vocalization.

In the meantime lips and epiglottis, various shaping appendages, and the hyoid anchorage for the muscles move in coordination to calibrate the consonants distinctly and to cut the [g] and [k] stops. We shape the sounds by motor command, and the entire tube obeys to produce the distinguishable phonemes which carry our thoughts thus encoded upon modifications of air currents. Our speaking efforts are usually pleasant exercises for speaker and listener alike, rendering us prone to speak for mere aesthetic pleasure even at times when we have little thought to convey.

We observe that children, when first learning to speak, mount their thoughts on words and sounds which they themselves comprehend, but which are not yet sculptured well enough to enable their parents and siblings to understand immediately. Children have a drive which makes them want to be understood. Consequently they keep trying until the listeners understand -- to the delight of both parties. The child is thus building its speech automatisms which settle into place quite rapidly, being shaped specifically to reproduce the mother tongue. Each new success brings delight to the child, who loves to repeat resonant vowels and calibrated consonants for sheer pleasure.

A mother cannot imprint her speech patterns upon the brain of her child, but she can stimulate the child to invent its own language. With her smile and approval she can encourage the child to imitate what it hears, and so stimulate its brain, nerves and muscles to learn the speech patterns of its native language.

I suspect - this is not science - that children, when testing their speech and learning to format vowels which resonate well when the speaking tube is set right, may come by accident or practice upon that formatting of the speech tube which best resonates the vowels like a trombone or base tuba. They love to repeat this pleasant and musical reverberation in the hollow of their properly shaped speaking tubes because they resonate well in the formatted pharynx and oral cavity. By repeating often what they love to hear, they build and adjust the neural pathways and musculature to "tune" their throats to produce sounds "in tune" at conscious command. Soon they are rewarded with a self-adjusting vowel formatting automatism which is in perfect tune. Similarly for the consonants and stops. They are helped in this process of developing automatisms specific to the native language by doting parents and siblings who share the delight of the little one when it hits the vowel tone perfectly, and cuts the consonants and stops intelligibly. As the child grows, the powers to invent ever new automatisms for foreign languages gradually decrease in range and elasticity. For example, try as they might, many Japanese adults have an enormous difficulty with distinguishing both the pronunciation and perception of our American English pronunciation of "R" and "L." To many, the sounds remain almost exactly the same, being indistinguishable even after many efforts of trying to learn a difference.

THE PRODUCTION OF SPEECH

How we perform our speech on the two-tube system is a marvel that overshadows the apparently simple mechanics of the tubal maneuvers as described above. With scarcely perceptible effort we set into action the 13 billion nerves to orchestrate the encoding upon air currents of the thoughts of our hearts and minds. The brain is indeed a marvel, about which geneticist Jerome Lejeune (now departed) records his amazement:

> Take first of all the macro and micro structure of the brain, for the most complex connecting network that we presently know on earth [measuring two hundred thousand kilometers in length, if one

calculates in neuro-tubules] to that extraordinary play of synapses which causes a flow of particles to be engulfed by the receptive membrane when a small vessel bursts and emits a chemical mediator (Lejeune 1989, 24).

When speaking, we maneuver our tubes and send a pressured airstream through them which originates in the lungs and is issued under pressure generated by the diaphragm bellows and surrounding musculature. By varying the tension of our drawn vocal cords we set the pitch of the tone. When we qualify and format these tonal frequencies of intermittent air jets by shaping and resonating them within the supralaryngeal tract, and exit this speech-calibrated stream of air, our neighbor can comprehend the thought which is in our mind; that thought which the nerves of the brain have translated into electro-chemical signals, which our speech organs have released into the air as articulated air pressure variance signals. If the recipient knows the language of the speaker, these air pressure signals carry a semantic code for the listener. The people who know us even recognize the individual resonance and clipped articulation of our voice, which has our personal trademark.

What we do by speaking is nothing short of the phenomenal. Eric H. Lennenberg, when recording three radio newscasters, found that they spoke an average of 5.7, 5.9, and 6.0 syllables per second. For each syllable there are about 2.4 phonemes, distinguishable sound-coded identities; that totals about fourteen phonemes per second (6 X 2.4). All the while we form and reform our air passage to resonate and articulate the sound. The passage from one phoneme into another -- its onset, the phone itself, and then the subsequent transition -- depends ultimately upon the differences in muscle adjustments. The brain gives the muscles their proper orders to contract, to relax, or to hold their tonus. At least one hundred muscles are engaged simultaneously. The brain therefore sends these fourteen hundred orders per second to produce the phonemes in rapid succession to the targeted 100 engaged muscles (see Lennenberg, 91-92). If we admire piano players who can play 16-20 notes per second, all the more do we marvel our speech automatisms with which may be doing up to 1400 articulations per second with perfect ease - 70 times faster than the flying fingers of the piano virtuoso.

The brain does not just fire off the fourteen hundred orders per second at random. It issues the electro-chemical neural transmissions in that magnitude of power and that order of sequence at which we are giving command. The arrival of the nerve's electro-chemical transmission at the target muscle must be in proper sequence, and its strength must stimulate the correct amplitude of the twitch of that muscle. The brain fires the signals from its motor strip terminal in a flurry of activity, subject to our conscious will to speak. Because some muscles are more distant from the source than others, the sequence of firing may need to be timed in reverse. Moreover, some of the nerves are thick and blitz the signal to the target muscle at about three hundred miles per hour, whereas other extremely fine nerves send the signal at a leisurely walking pace of 1.5 miles per hour. The brain must compute for distance and speed by firing the signals to coordinate the pull of the muscles to be exactly on split-second schedule to produce speech in proper order. Sometimes things get mixed up or go awry, and the ear, which monitors what is happening, admonishes us to correct ourselves and repeat, this time correctly. The short term memory keeps constant tabs on the on-going conversation and keeps our thoughts connected.

We can do all this with apparent ease and embellish what we say with added elegance of sparkling eyes, smiling face, and lilting voice when we deliver pleasant thoughts. Or, we can express displeasure by making the voice grate and rasp, by curling the lips, tweaking the nose, arching the eyebrows, clenching the fists, bulging the neck, erecting the hair, flushing the face scarlet, and flashing bolts of lightning from the eyes. Whether we speak with cooing love or with a towering rage, we can authenticate our intended meaning with these additional signs of communication.

Of course the brain doesn't pioneer all this every time we initiate verbal conversation. The brain is not an amateur but a seasoned professional, performing well after much practice. Our speech capabilities began to develop early, taking off at high speed around the age of two. The wiring of the brain for language ability is perfected only gradually:

> Recent experimental data indicate that the acquisition of speech by children also involves genetically transmitted innate neural mechanisms that structure the production and perception of speech. Linguistic ability, particularly phonetic ability, appears to involve a 'critical period' in which a child must be exposed to a language in a productive manner (Lieberman 1984, 332).

The primary language learning season lasts into the early teens, after which time new languages appear to be wired into the existing apparatus, as secondary circuits are plugged into primary circuits already in place. We ask next what the fossil record may reveal about the time when human speech began on earth; not just rudimentary speech, but the full ability to support thought and responsible human action.

Chapter 3

PRE-HOMO SAPIENS NOT IN EDEN

Very ancient fossils of hominid skulls, skeletons, and dentures, sometimes found together with fabricated stone tools, indicate that intelligent human beings inhabited our globe for a long time before we came on the scene. Some of the fossils date back to several million years ago. Museums exhibit them or their replicas, and standard anthropological texts describe details. We would be ostriches hiding our heads in the sands if we pretend that these are not real.

I viewed some of the original objects which the Leakey family members had discovered, which are now on exhibit in the National Museum in Nairobi, Kenya. To my unpracticed eye they appeared as genuine as they are claimed to be. I also marveled at the nearly complete fossil of "Lucy" said to be 3.5 million years old which Donald Johanson and team discovered in the region of Hadar in Ethiopia. The question arises, though, whether fossils which date back several million years are relics of descendants of the Adam and Eve of the Bible, the ones who committed original sin. I lean to the opinion that these very ancient humans who are now extinct, were not the ancestors who committed original sin, the ones from whom we are descended.

Among anthropological exhibits in museums today, replicas of the shapely fossils of "Lucy" deservedly enjoy a place of honor. The story telling how two scientists found her fossils on top of the sand in the Afar region of Ethiopia is related dramatically in the book Johanson-Edey, *Lucy, The Beginnings Of Humankind*, 16-17. A reading of the book reveals much about the thoroughness with which these scientists went about their work. Three years after the discovery Donald Johanson and Timothy White completed their study of the fossils. They finally decided that she could not be human. As Johanson wrote: "She was so odd that there was no question about her not being a human. She simply wasn't. She was too little. Her brain was too small. Her jaw was the wrong shape. With these "primitive" traits staring me in the face, I interpreted other things in her dentition as primitive also, as pointing away from the human condition and back in the direction of apes" (*Lucy,* 258). But she did walk erect on two feet, and her dentures identify her to be in the hominid line, clearly distinguished from the chimpanzee and ape lines. The strata in which they found her diminutive fossils were eventually identified as "close to 3.5 million years old" (*Lucy*, 202-203), a million years more ancient than the oldest stone tools discovered to date.

Present data indicates that the line of humans we call Habilis made stone tools 2.5 million years ago (at Hadar in Ethiopia, see *Lucy*, 231). This indicates - at least to me it indicates - that the population who made them had intelligence and freedom, an immaterial and immortal soul. With forethought and planning they fashioned stone working tools. Man and wife likely shared work. Groups would organize to divide labors, to hunt as a unit, to protect each other and to share food, and so develop culture and speech abilities.

Louis Leakey found a nearly 2 million year old fossil skull in association with stone tools at Olduvai in 1959. The tools were pieces of lava and quartz which must have been brought to the site from three miles away since that was their closest source. The collection includes crude rounded pebble tools, but also advanced tools. A site at the bottom of the gorge contains eleven different kinds of stone implements, such as engraving-gouging tools, quadrilateral 'chisels,' large and small scrapers, and other special purpose tools generally made of difficult to work lava and quartz. The Leakeys also found what they interpret to be a semicircular wall at Olduvai which, they speculate, served as a shelter and windbreak. It has been dated at 2 million years old, plus-minus 280,000 years (Victor Barnouw, *Physical Anthropology and Anthropology*, 118; see also *Lucy*, 229; and Bernard G. Campbell, *Humankind Emerging*, Sixth edition, 238 ff.).

The tool makers, who presumably hunted animals for food and fashioned their skins into clothing, who also built shelters, undoubtedly exercised considerable social coordination, which is an index of human speech ability.

But how well were these pre-Homo Sapiens people able to speak, we ask. Scientist Philip Lieberman provides information, which to non-scientist myself is convincing, that Homo Sapiens is the first in the fossil record with the cranial morphology which can indicate the presence of our modern type of fully developed speech organs (Lieberman 1984, 256 ff.). On this basis I see no possibility that the ancient Homo Habilis who made tools 2.5 million years ago was of the tribe of our Adam who committed original sin. He could not speak well enough to have an adult sense of responsibility. He could make tools, he could hunt, he could socialize with others, but so long as he could not speak with modern facility, God would not hold him responsible for grievous matters. His still underdeveloped speech abilities did not capacitate him to reflect sufficiently about responsibilities, nor to decide with adult finality. The same must have been the case with Homo Erectus who follows Habilis in the fossil record. The 1.6 million years ago fossil of a twelve year old Erectus boy found by the Richard Leakey team on the shores of Lake Turkana in Africa (cf. Leakey 1985, p. 629), resembles our body-build. But his basi-cranium indicates that he did not have our modern type of speech organs. The same is true about the other fossils of Erectus.

Peoples of the Erectus type are said to have fanned out from Africa into the areas where Italy, Spain, France, Hungary and other countries are today, as well as to India, Java, and north into China (see map, Campbell, p. 308). The diggings in Zhoukoutien (formerly spelt Choukutien), near Peking in China indicate that Erectus lived there for a very long time. Recent Chinese researchers date human occupation of the caves between 230,000-500,000 years ago (Campbell, 286). The findings give us considerable insight into their type of living:

> The continuing excavations produced thousands of stone tools. There were simple choppers with only a few chips removed, but they were made to a pattern. In the largest cave that was explored, 100,000 stone tools and fragments, most of quartz, were found. Some of them lay with charred bits of wood and bone. From this it was concluded that Sinanthropus had mastered the use of fire. The ash of some deposits were enormous in quantity, 22 feet deep - dramatic evidence that appeared to indicate that the fires were not permitted to die out. The bones and antlers of thousands of animals

were present in the deposits. Nearly three-quarters of them belonged to deer; there were also bones of giant sheep, zebra, pigs, buffalo, rhinoceros, monkeys, bisons, elephant, and even such river dwellers as the otter. Among these were scattered the bones of predators, of bear, hyena, wolves, fox, badger, leopard and other cats, and of humans. All these bones came from species that are now extinct (Campbell, 285).

These people probably spent much of the day hunting and gathering, and then spent the evenings around the fires. All this indicates that they must have had a considerable division of labor, that they could communicate adequately with each other, and exercised considerable technical skill. They may very well have developed significant human culture and manners, and perhaps discussed the meaning of life as they ate their meals and warmed themselves around the fires.

Carl C. Swisher III of the Berkeley Geochronology Center recently made the significant claim that Homo Erectus lived in Java between 27,000 and 53,000 years ago, and that Homo Sapiens arrived at the island about 40,000 years ago. The two types apparently co-existed until Erectus became extinct. "The key difference between Erectus and Sapiens was in the brain. The Sapiens brain is about 25 percent larger and this may have been the difference between the survival of one species and the demise of the other" (AP, Washington, 17 December 1996).

"Homo Antecessor" whom scientists claim to have lived about 800,000 years ago, is said to have some features which resemble Neanderthals, others more akin to Homo

Sapiens. His bulky lower jaw, primitive teeth and ridged brow favor Neanderthals, his cheekbones and his canine fossa favor Homo Sapiens. The Spanish anthropological team who discovered 50 fossilized specimens in northern Spain during 1995 and 1996 believe they are ancestors of three branches of peoples, Homo Heidelbergensis, the Neanderthals and Homo Sapiens. They postulate that all three types lived simultaneously about 500,000 years ago, but since 250,000 ago only Homo Sapiens survived (*Daily Yomiuri,* January 20, 1998). (But we saw just above the claim of Swisher that Homo Erectus lived in Java up to 27,000 years ago. The human family tree continues to be refined as new discoveries are made.)

DEFICIENT IN SPEECH

While anthropologists continue to modify the family tree in accordance with successive recent discoveries, we assume that Lieberman and associates will logically abide by their postulate that Homo Sapiens along could have possessed the advanced type of language abilities comparable to our own. The extended length of the palate of all hominids other than Homo Sapiens is too long to allow space for our two-tube airway system. Therefore, the other hominids can have had only the standard one-tube system and were consequently unable to do our [a], [i], and [u] vowels; our [g] and [k] stops; and the fine calibration which enables us to produce so many recognizable phonemes at high speed.

Were one to insist on putting into the other hominids tongues as thick as those of Homo Sapiens, and to have equally long oral and pharyngeal sections, we would make them into monsters with the larynx (Adam's apple) in the chest instead of in the neck. The long palates of Australopithecus, Habilis, Erectus, and Neanderthal fossils indicate that they supported vocal tracts "in which the tongue is long and thin and is positioned almost entirely within the oral cavity" (Lieberman 1984, 296).

These scientists do not claim that the earlier hominids were totally unable to speak homan languages, but they point out that our modern type of speech organs simply don't fit into earlier hominid fossils. They reconstructed a Neanderthal supralaryngeal vocal tract and found that it could not generate the formant frequency patterns of the vowels and stops mentioned above (Liberman 1984, 318). The advantage of superior speech abilities was likely a factor in the rapid development of Homo Sapiens and probably of his replacement of Neanderthal (see ibid. 333)

We are today one human race of the species Homo Sapiens, spread over the globe, all able to intermarry and have offspring. Adam and Eve were originators of our race, then, but probably not ancestors of the Neanderthals. Bernard G. Campbell, in *Humankind Emerging*, notes that the Cro-Magnon population, who were Homo Sapiens, lived contemporaneously with Neanderthals, but that the two groups remained apart:

> Archaeologists believed that there was no cultural connection between Neanderthal and Cro-Magnon peoples. The stone tools of the Cro-Magnons seemed markedly more sophisticated than Neanderthal implements. And when archaeologists dug down through successive layers in caves, they sometimes found sterile layers between the Neanderthal deposits and the deposits left by Cro-Magnons, indicating that no one had occupied the cave

for a time. These layers containing no sign of human occupation were interpreted as proof that the Neanderthals had become extinct without having given rise to their successors in Western Europe (Campbell, 381).

ETERNAL DESTINY OF NEANDERTHALS AND OTHERS

The non-Homo Sapiens people of ancient times, then, may well have enjoyed life intensely much as children do today before they reach adulthood. They could speak and think to some extent and carry on social life in conformity with their comparatively limited intellectual powers. Their power to think abstractly indicates that they had immaterial and immortal souls which do not die. What about their eternal destiny?

The Lord has not seen fit to reveal this to us. But we know that every single person whom He once creates, lives forever after. This is true of all persons, whether they are children or adults, whether born or unborn. We know also that God loves everything He has made, and that He is infinitely good. We entrust the non-Homo Sapiens hominids to His goodness, just as we entrust to Him the children whom He has created and who die without Baptism before they could be born, or who died after birth but before reaching the use of reason.

HOMO SAPIENS: THE MAN IN EDEN

The Homo Sapiens skull and connecting backbone which are ours can obviously accommodate our type of speech organs. We assume that Homo Sapiens developed intellectually over a span of years, until he reached the threshold of mature deliberation, capable of assuming the responsibilities of Eden. When the fullness of time came, God "put the man whom he had formed" (Gen 3:8) into the Garden of Eden which He had planted for him. There God revealed Himself to our Adam in a supernatural manner, and constituted him in the supernatural state of holiness and justice.

This means that God irradiated Adam's mind with the divine light of infused faith, capacitating him to see light with God's light. His natural human intelligence took a quantum leap when natural truths were suffused with the background light of infused faith. God also explained to him the chief truths about man and the universe by the primal revelation, which was given to him as the founder of the race which God now specially favored. The rest of the Homo Sapiens people -- assuming that there were such -- and the Neanderthal groups either continued to live genetically isolated from the Eden people, or they were already extinct. At any rate, only the descendants of the Eden people remain on the earth today. We are all descendants of those to whom God gave the gifts of holiness and justice in Eden, whereas all other human populations have become extinct.

CONCLUSION

The writer has become convinced, upon reading Lieberman and others, that it is correct to conclude that our Adam and Eve are Homo Sapiens people who began our race. The fossil record gives us a general idea of how long ago they lived: it could have been any time after the speech organs and neurological substratum were in place -- perhaps in the neighborhood of 200,000 years ago.

Chapter 4

A COUPLE OR A POPULATION?

Among those who believe that the our human bodies descended from living animal origins, some are more comfortable with the idea that our race began with a population rather than with a single couple. Though the teaching office of the Catholic Church may not be definitively opposed to the population concept, the current teaching points to a couple and not to a popuation, at least until reasons to change become convincing. Pope Pius XII found this difficulty with the population theory:

> It is not at all apparent how such a view (polygenism) can be reconciled with the data which the sources of revealed truth and the documents of the Church propose concerning original sin, namely, that it originates from a sin truly committed by one Adam, is transmitted to all through generation and is in each person, proper to him (cf. Rom 5:12-19); Encyclical <u>Humani Generis</u>, 1950; DS 3896; Dupuis 420).

Theologians feel challenged to explore ways in which polygenism can be reconciled with the doctrine of original sin when they see this explanation of Pope Pius XII. The words: "for it is not at all apparent ..." leave the door at least partially open for further study.

THEORIES FAVORING A POPULATION

An explanation designed to bridge the gap between supporters of polygenism vs. advocates of a single couple origin made by Z. Alszegy and M. Flick received considerable attention when first announced. They proposed that one single couple who had already achieved full use of reason was responsible for this sin. This couple formed part of a larger group who had not yet achieved full moral responsibility. These others are presented as being in a state of undeveloped childhood. According to the testimony of Holy Scripture the first man is to be viewed as a corporate person, whose decision becomes the fate of the group; and thus the actual sin of a single person could become the hereditary sin of the rest of the people. I am not aware that this theory has received widespread acceptance. Fr. Ferdinand Holboeck (p.149) rightly observes that this and similar theories do not exceed the value of inconclusive speculation.

If I understand the above theory correctly, it is not much of an improvement over the older explanation of Thomas, namely that the first couple sinned personally, and the rest of humanity inherited their sin. To me the explanation appears artificially contrived. It is apparently designed to meet the opinion of those who hold to the theory of human evolution from animal stock, and who believe that the science of genetics would demand a larger gene pool for the origin of Homo Sapiens than one single couple. There is no unanimity among scientists about this. Geneticist Jerome Lejeune, (see below) held quite the opposite opinion, namely that a genetic novelty spreads more easily from a single source than from a dissipated group.

AN ISOLATED GENE POOL

We may speculate that our Adam and Eve ancestors were born into an existing population, but broke away from them and launched our race in isolation from the parent group. It is not at all inconceivable that a single pair of humans, or a small population, can become isolated from the rest of humanity in a hunter-gatherer kind of social situation. Only recently, for example, a small tribe of hunter-gatherers in the mountains of New Guinea, isolated into an area on the border of the Enga highlands and the Province of Madang, contacted our SVD missionaries to ask for help. Their group of only 302 persons feared that they would die out if they received no outside help. They had known practically nothing about the rest of the world before 1983 (SVD *Arnoldus,* January/February 1983, p.8). If this group was isolated from the rest of the inhabitants of New Guinea from as long as their memory goes back, we can reasonably suppose that an Adam and Eve could detach themselves from the rest of humanity terminally.

Nor is it inconceivable that populations living prior to our Homo Sapiens race became extinct. We know of Australopithecus hominids from 4 million year old fossils (see *Lucy,* 202) but they are no more today. Fossils of Homo Habilis, of Homo Erectus, and of Neanderthal tell us the story that they once existed, but are no more. We know also that many nations of the Homo Sapiens race once flourished in great numbers, but have now become extinct. Corrado Gini counted up a number of nations once demographically numerous which are now extinct:

> Examples of the progressive decadence of primitive populations, apparently doomed to certain death, are very numerous. They are to be met with in all continents; in the northern regions of Asia, of Europe, and America, the Australian continent, and the Malayan and Oceanian archipelagoes, the is-

lands of the coast of Indo-China, and the interior of
the peninsula, a place in Palestine, central Africa,
some of the Indian reservations of Canada and of
the United States, the virgin forests of the Ama-
zons, and in the extreme south of the American
continent (Gini, p. 51).

Biological decay, believes Gini, is the principle cause of
their death, but diseases, abuses, wars, violent social changes may be the final critical factor. During relatively modern
times many of the Australian hunter-gatherers were
decimated or wiped out by diseases contracted from white
men for which they had not developed resistance. The
same is true of American Indians of a hundred years ago,
and of Amazonians today. It is also known that internecine
wars sometimes wiped out competitive groups of hunter
gatherers. Climatic conditions also played their role, and
some believe that the Neanderthal people were wiped out
when glaciers invaded their habitats, or when Homo
Sapiens perhaps eliminated them.

Finally, it is not at all inconceivable that our Adam and Eve
people would remain genetically isolated from other populations, either for geographic reasons, or because of social
and linguistic barriers. Linguistic and cultural barriers can
isolate genetic pools from each other as effectively as
impassable mountain ranges, vast oceans, and impenetrable
forests.

POPULATION THEORIES AND GENETICS

The theory of human evolution from an animal origin is
compatible with the above theoretical scenario. After the
original pair had become genetically isolated from their

parent gene pool, their own genetic endowment could give rise to the vast population of the world today with its evidently rich genetic endowments.

Geneticist Jerome Lejeune, for example, observed that if our race is a new species, then a single couple to start the species is more logical than a group of people or a population:

> Indeed I am of the opinion that the whole chromosomal mechanics require that every species must have arisen in an extremely inbred and small population. The calculus from genetics shows that the optimal solution would be to start with a unique couple, carrier of the chromosomal novelty in the homozygous state (Lejeune, private correspondence, 19 February 1987, permission obtained).

Note that the eminent geneticist, now deceased, did not claim here that Homo Sapiens IS a new species. He observes only that IF ours is a new species, then the calculus from genetics would point to a couple rather than to a corporate population as its base of origin.

Genetic calculations also practically exclude the possibility that a Homo Sapiens race would begin spontaneously in several parts of the world. Rather, there can be only one source of our race, only one cross-over from the animal world into human society. That is, if a species-specific mutation from animal to human, or from one human species to another, occurred in Africa, for example, and another occurred in a genetically isolated population in Asia or elsewhere, the two new species would not be identical. They would not be capable of cross-fertilization to beget offspring. A concept that multiple lines evolved into a new species separately in genetically isolated situations, and that the species was the identical and single species of Homo Sapiens is, in all likelihood, not defensible by genetic calculus. Our Homo Sapiens race, therefore, if it is specifically different from Homo Habilis, Erectus, and Neanderthal, began at one place only, not in several and independent isolated gene pools.

MITOCHONDRIAL DNA CONVERGES

Newsweek of January 11, 1988 described studies which point to a convergence of our family tree. The tree converges toward an African woman who lived about two hundred thousand years ago. The DNA examined in the research is not that which is inside the nucleus of human cells but outside of it in mitochondrion compartments. This is inherited only from the mother, not from the father, and is therefore useful for tracing family lines through the female ancestors. This mitochondrial DNA is not scrambled with that of the father, as is the case with the DNA which is within the nucleus of cells. This provides it with a marker by which changes can be traced in generations of women.

Minute changes in the mitochondrial DNA occur during the course of time, and these changes can be traced, step by step, back to the source of the novelty. The changes diverge in different directions among populations that are genetically isolated from each other.

The Berkeley group who did the study obtained mtDNA by collecting placentas of women in America with ancestors from Africa, Europe, the Middle East, and Asia, and from Aborigines in Australia and New Guinea. They found two main categories of the mtDNA, one found only in some babies of a certain population of recent African descent, and a second found in all others, including other Africans. They concluded that the former line is the oldest, that all the other lines branched off from it. The researchers assumed a steady rate of mutations and by this molecular calculus came upon the original woman. She lived in Africa, they say, some two hundred thousand years ago (a range between 140,000 and 290,000 years ago). That would locate the single and unique mother of our entire present human race in Africa.

Professor Lucotte of the Sorbonne, Paris, conducted studies on the DNA of the Y sex chromosome which is exclusively male. A similar branching pattern emerged. It converged on a male ancestor of our race who was also African (Campbell 447). But the results are admittedly tentative and highly controversial. If these findings are true they point to Africa as the locus of the origins of our contemporary race. These studies do not indicate by themselves, however, that a monogamous couple launched our race.

Be that as it may, we have an independent source of knowledge by which we know that our primal ancestors were monogamous. Christ testified in Matthew chapter nineteen that "in the beginning" the union of one husband and wife was arranged by God, and only later did divorce and re-marriage come into practice. This saying of Christ evidently describes fact not symbolism, for Christ made God's initial arrangement of monogamy to be the model on which He restored Christian marriage to the pristine condition. The possibility remains, of course, that there was an original population with numerous families all of which were monogamous. Christ's statement, by itself, does not exclude that possibility.

THEOLOGICAL INDICATIONS FAVOR A COUPLE

Do theologians have reasons to conclude that it was one single couple who began our present human race, and to exclude even a small genetically isolated population of monogamous couples? Luke traces the genealogy of Jesus back to an initial ancestor "Adam, son of God" (3:38). This single source has symbolic significance, it appears, for the Evangelist makes quite an issue about the ancestry of Christ. The beginning of the genealogical tree is Adam. If Adam was not this specified individual but an unknown and unnamed person within an initial general population then Luke's superb narrative would lose its punch line. Luke's genealogy has a rhythmic regression through seventy-six generations of ancestors. We know many of them from the Bible as colorful individuals. The line of royal ancestry crescendoes to a climax in Adam, son of God:

> Jesus, when he began his ministry was about thirty years of age, being the son (as was thought) of Joseph, the son of Heli, the son of Matthat, the son of Levi, the son of Melchi... etc. etc.... the son of Mahalaleel, the son of Cainan, the son of Enos, the son of Seth, the son of Adam, the son of God (Lk 3:23-38).

It would be an anti-climax to read instead at the end: " the son of Seth, the son of an unidentified parent in an initial population." Luke's charming genealogy builds up an esteem for Christ in the reader, who already knows the Adam well from the pages of the Bible, the one who is

Christ's human ancestor as well as our own. Luke marks us as relatives of the human Christ, who shares His ancestry with us. We would extinguish and lose one very significant detail of the heritage of our Faith, I believe, if we would replace our "Adam" of Bible with a "Conglomerate Population" of science. Even from a literary standpoint, a banal "conglomerate population" does not stand up to the exquisite climax of Luke's "Adam, the son of God." It would be an anti-climax, a departure from the elegant style of Luke and from his accustomed minute care about meaningful details. As for myself, I opt for my family tree to start with Adam, and would hate to change him for a nameless parent belonging to an initial population.

Two significant theological considerations converge, I believe: Luke states that the ancestor was Adam. Matthew states that he was monogamous. Put the two together, and I believe we have a good case for concluding that our race descended from one monogamous couple.

Paul marks a dramatic comparison between Christ our new spiritual father, and Adam our father in the flesh. Christ is the single source of supernatural life, Adam stands opposite Christ as the single source of our race. Paul's comparison loses its punch when we oppose Christ against an initial population. The magnificent passage of Rom 5:12-21 is well focused as we read it: "For if many died through one man's trespass, much more have the grace of God and the free gift of the grace in that one man Jesus Christ abounded for many" (Rom 5:15). The focus would be diffused if we would read instead: "For if many died through one initial population's trespass..." The figure of Adam as the ancestor and figure of Christ has a significance in symbolism which likely makes it a part of our deposit of faith. Since

Adam is a figure of Christ, he is one man, not a population. The argument is not conclusive but it is persuasive.

Finally, from a practical point of view, a corporate sin by an enclosed population does not fit into the picture of the first offense of man against God very well. Some might suggest that an entire group might have sinned in an agreement of mutiny and rebellion. But if a population committed the sin as one corporation, would that same population also repent as one corporation? According to the Bible, Adam and Eve made their peace with God after the Fall. Would an entire population do that? Would they all sin, then all repent, as though they were a mechanically controlled machinery of robots? That strains our sense of credibility. It is easier to believe that one couple sinned and then repented, than to assume that an entire population sinned today and then an entire population repented tomorrow.

CONCLUSION

The final word may not yet have been spoken, but as things stand today, we have no compelling reason to disown a monogamous couple, whom we conventionally name Adam and Eve, as our primal human ancestors. We would not improve the narration of the Bible on the one hand, nor scientific theory on the other, by naming Adam and Eve a population.

Chapter 5

THE SIN AS TOLD IN GENESIS

It is not by fortuitous oversight that the Bible hastens to relate the story of original sin on its page two. The arrangement is designed to project sin as a high profile truth of the faith. The first page relates truth Number One: God is our Creator. The second teaches truth Number Two: we are sinners and Christ is our Redeemer. Page one of the New Testament then follows through with the narration of the coming of the Redeemer.

Chapters 1-3 of Genesis plus the Gospel story about Christ form the very basis of revealed religion for a vast part of mankind, for the millions of Jews, Christians, and Muslims in particular. Genesis 1-3 is known to almost every one in the world to some extent, even to those who do not yet know Christ and His will to redeem us. These chapters of Genesis continue to generate belief in the Creator God who cares about humans, and who gives them a code of proper conduct which He expects them to follow.

If we ask whether the first chapters of Genesis narrate factual history, or whether the content is didactic mythology, we pose the problem too simplistically. History and symbol are both there, but the sacred author clothes history in symbol and sacralizes myth with revelation. There is history, very basic history, but just where symbol ceases and naked chronology emerges is not all clear to us. Writing of chronological history was invented only a few thousand years ago, whereas the events of Genesis 1-11 bear the marks of oral tradition which humans may have been passing down to succeeding generations in an unbroken thread of legend from time immemorial -- perhaps in some form even from the very day on which original sin was committed; the event which we have good reason to believe occurred maybe 200,000 years ago, give or take handfuls of some tens of thousands.

It is difficult to find a more succinct and satisfying explanation to identify what is history in Genesis, and what is symbol, than this passage from the Encyclical Letter Humani Generis promulgated by Pope Pius XII in 1950:

> The first eleven chapters of Genesis...do in some true sense come under the heading of history; in what exact sense, it is for the further study of exegetes to determine. These chapters have a naive, symbolic way of speaking, well suited to the understanding of primitive people. But they do disclose important truths, upon which the attainment of our eternal salvation depends, and they do also give a popular description of the origin of the human race and of the chosen people. It may be true that the ancient authors of sacred history drew some of their material from current popular stories. So much may be granted. But it must be remembered that they did so under the impulse of divine inspiration which preserved them from all error in selecting and assessing the documents they used (trans. of Jaques Dupuis in *The Christian Faith*, No.239, hereinafter referenced as Dupuis).

In brief, the sacred writers were artists who could make the truth shine with splendor through symbol and even myth, in a manner designed to make the truths intelligible to children as well as to adults. In this the sacred writers

are by no means less artful than was Aesop who constructed homespun fables pleasant in the telling, very
meaningful for teaching about life, often making animals
do the talking to heighten the drama of the foibles of
people. Genesis, however, is a sacred narration on a "distinctly different level from" profane writings (Humani
Generis, Dupuis, ibid.). We study Genesis, then, with
reverence and at the same time we search for the truth
clothed in symbols.

The nature of the sin of Adam and Eve as described in
Genesis is raw disobedience to a command of God. Among
the trees which God had planted in the Garden of Eden,
two were special: the tree of life and the tree of the knowledge of what is good and what is bad. God put the tree of
life into the midst of the garden, but the other tree was
also located where it was easily accessible. God then gave
this command:

> And the Lord God commanded the man, saying,
> "You may freely eat of every tree of the garden;
> but of the tree of the knowledge of good and evil
> you shall not eat, for in the day that you eat of it
> you shall die" Gen 2:16-17.

The test was not an ordinance laid down by God as though
to thump His chest and exhibit arbitrary power. The ordinance confirmed what was already written into created
nature. Adam had no right to treat good and evil alike, as
though there were no difference between the two. God's
injunction seconded and confirmed Adam's intuition. Adam
could already know, at least in a dimly intuitive manner,
that he is always invited to help himself to the tree of life -
- to nourish himself with what is positive and good, with

God's grace. He could likewise know that it was obligatory to abstain from engaging indiscriminately in evil conduct as though there were no difference between good and evil, as though truth did not exist, and as though God would not care about his moral behavior.

Adam already possessed an obligation to honor and obey his own natural intuitions about goodness and truth. It is not right for a man to treat good and evil as though they were the same, as though both grew from the same tree. This intuited obligation God now confirmed and made unmistakably clear by the revealed commandment. The test was whether Adam would obey his conscience after God had improved its power to judge correctly with revelation; and had suffused his mind with the light of faith. God had spoken a "Thou shalt not." Adam's action was raw disobedience. He was inexperienced to be sure, but disobey he did, and God held him responsible for the misdeed.

Some exegetes also find hints in the narrative that the author had an additional agenda in mind, namely to dissuade the Israelites from taking part in fertility rites of the Canaanite religion. The serpent which appears on the scene thereafter was a sex symbol associated with the worship of the god Baal and the goddess Apo, both fertility deities (cf. Bruce Vawter, 181). The fig leaf detail may suggest a connection with fertility rites. Some theorize, therefore, that the author of Genesis knit details into the story designed to dissuade the Israelites from assisting in fertility rites.

Whatever merit that theory may have, the Genesis story is not primarily a lesson in chastity. For readers of the Bible today the story of the Fall is first and foremost a lesson that man the creature has an obligation to obey God his Creator. Man must be true to himself in his actions; he is an image of God, and by natural bent acts like himself when he acts as a member of God's family ought to act; over and above this he must obey God who clarifies by revelation what man already knows less clearly by powers of reason. Man must obey, must do good and avoid evil, or take the consequences.

We all feel a bit of empathy with Adam and Eve so far, curious about what might happen if they do disobey. God had told them that one of the fruit trees was off limits for them, namely the "tree of the knowledge of good and evil." But what fruit is ever sweeter than forbidden fruit? And what grass can ever be greener than grass across the fence? The prohibition was a temptation, a challenge, a gauntlet lying there waiting to be picked up.

The Genesis text indicates that God issued the prohibition by a revelation -- that is, by a word spoken to man by God. God was ordering them to follow His instructions, to obey Him in this matter, regardless of what they might wish to choose. Their motive for complying would be faith in God the Speaker, over and above a conclusion of reason. God was asking them to grasp His invisible hand and walk with Him, without looking back at what their own preferences might be.

Everyman, however, lusts for independence. We want to make the laws ourselves, create good and bad by fiat of the will, explore the dangerous and unknown. We are fascinated with lighting matches when we are children, and dream impossible ambitions even when we are old.

Shall we yield to God who claims obedience because He is Lord and Creator of the universe? Such is the test put to Adam and Eve. And such is the test of Everyman throughout mortal life. Philosopher Peter Henrichi describes reason when it seeks to be detached from its anchor in truth:

> Amongst the false gods that man has devised for himself, there is none that has usurped the place of the true God more gravely than reason. The French Revolution put reason on its altars ... "the supreme eye of reason, which has come to scatter the clouds of darkness." But there is no need to go back through the centuries. We know from our daily experience how apt reason is to be substituted for the Holy Spirit...

> Reason, the faculty that directs human action, operates by drawing its conclusions from the premises that it posits, in this way fashioning its own system. By its very nature, reason wants always to be right. It is argumentative and loath to let itself be convinced. Jealous of its autonomy, reason upholds the independence of man, a rational animal, who derives his dignity from it - not to mention his pride... "Vainglorious reason" is par excellence the instrument of human pride, an instrument by the aid of which "God is dispensed with in an atmosphere of haughty disdain" (Henrichi, p. 638).

Saint Augustine (354-430) assumes that Adam and Eve must have sinned by pride as a prelude to the final Fall:

> For the evil act (original sin) had never been done had not an evil will preceded it. And what is the

origin of our evil will but pride? For "pride is the beginning of sin" (Ecclus 10:13). And what is pride but the craving for undue exaltation? And this is undue exaltation, when the soul abandons Him to whom it ought to cleave as its end, and becomes a kind of end to itself (*City of God,* 14:13).

Though pride entered the sin, the author of Genesis wants us to know that very commonplace human drives were involved: an appetite for food, plus curiosity, all topped by confused and unwise ambition. Readers easily empathize with Adam and Eve, knowing similar movements in themselves. The sacred author highlights three kinds of temptations confronting Eve: the fruit on the tree whets her appetite, esoteric gnosis promises elite mysticism, choice of what is good and what is evil would make her creative, like God. These temptations are common to all mankind. As John wrote: "For all that is in the world, the lust of the flesh and the lust of the eyes and the pride of life, is not of the Father" (1 John 2:16). The sacred author is teaching the entire human race, by means of this narration, about temptations which we all meet.

The expression "knowledge of good and evil" is an umbrella term to cover universal moral knowledge, from A to Z, from top to bottom, from horizon to horizon. By possessing knowledge of good and bad Eve would gain dominion over it. She would decide what is for her a good, what is for her an evil. She would be morally autonomous, without need of direction and instruction from outside, from any source other than the self. It points to what Pope John Paul II recently called a "'creative' understanding of moral conscience," an exaltation of freedom almost to the point of idolatry (Veritatis Splendor, No. 54).

A creative conscience rejects obedience to God and en-
thrones arbitrary choice as supreme, as untouchable, as
god. Such is the final temptation which the serpent whis-
pered to Eve: "You will be like God, knowing good and
evil."

Another tree stood in the middle of paradise, the tree of
life. From this tree Adam and Eve were allowed to eat. It is
the tree of moral correctness. God thereby invited them to
take the high moral ground, to live according to the moral
pattern which God laid out for them. But Eve, and Adam
beside her, were not standing under that tree now. There
were out exploring to find something more exciting.

THE FALL AS NARRATED IN GENESIS

Enter, the serpent. This is the primordial revelation in the
Bible that an enemy of mankind is on the loose. That this
despoiler is introduced as a serpent is an insightful bit of
artistry in the text. Almost universally, humans think lowly
about snakes. Wet, slimy, fire in the eye, forked tongue,
hissing noise, cruel jaws, poison of fang, lacking sentiment
-- snakes have few friends.

This particular snake exhibits consummate serpentine
craft. Eve is no match for it. The beguiler begins its talk in
a friendly and sympathetic manner. The first greeting is
baited to trap Eve into a dialogue. Eve owed reverence to
God, to whom she should have turned for help. She should
have turned to her husband to get help and advice. She
should have turned her back to the serpent to avoid meeting this trial all by herself alone. Instead, she conversed
with the serpent, God's enemy. It was already an insult to
the Lord God.

The serpent had evidently cased the place before. It knew about God's prohibition against eating the forbidden fruit, but lied about it: "Did God say, 'You shall not eat of any tree in the garden?'" Eve corrected the error, but then added a bit of untruth to the prohibition to make it appear unreasonable and arbitrary: "God said, 'You shall not eat of the fruit of the tree which is in the midst of the garden, neither shall you touch it lest you die.'" There are two untruths here: it was the tree of life which stood in the "midst of the garden" (Gen 2:9). Eve had relocated what was of greater interest for herself; she regarded the bad tree as the midst of the garden. For Eve it was evidently in the central place, absorbing lustful attention. Second, God had not forbidden them to "touch" the tree. That bit of exaggeration originated with Eve.

The serpent's velvet-smooth promises were exactly what Eve's ears were itching to hear: "You will not die. For God knows that when you eat of it your eyes will be opened, and you will be like God, knowing good and evil." A great promise. Eve got carried away by the dream. She fell fast and hard. She likewise seduced her husband to do as she had done: "She took the fruit and ate; and she also gave some to her husband, and he ate."

St. Irenaeus (c. 125-c.203) observes that the two were still inexperienced, for God had not made them wise nor holy beyond the range of their early condition (*Adversus Haereses* IV,38,1). Adam was simply too immature at the time to live like a practiced and holy adult: "God had the power at the beginning to grant perfection to man; but as the latter (Adam) was only recently created, he could not possibly have received it...or retained it" (IV,38,2). The shock of their initial defeat awakened them and stimulated them to grow up. "Humankind needed to grow accustomed to bearing divinity" through trial and gradual maturation (III,20,2). Irenaeus scolds us for wanting to be holy instantly and without effort. He has little respect for holiness that did not mature through corresponding effort: "Things which fall into our lap and things acquired after much effort are not cherished in the same way" (IV, 37,7). For Irenaeus, the Adam and Eve who fell when still inexperienced, but who bravely rose again to live more wisely, are an example for all of us to follow.

An anti-climax follows the sin: God did not strike them with instant physical death, contrary to what they might have feared because He had told them: "In the day that you eat of it you shall die." But they didn't fall down physically and die. The sacred author is an artist. We are supposed to do some thinking on our own to solve what he leaves unsaid. God had stated clearly that they would die in the day of the eating. As we shall see, St. Augustine solved the problem by stating that they died spiritually on that day, and physically later. When they sinned, they died spiritually (*City of God* 13:23). The Council of Trent, as we shall also see, defined that Adam died a spiritual death as a result of his sin. The sacred author teaches the message cryptically by describing how they had been friends with God before the sin, but feared Him after the sin. He invites us to ponder the matter deeply.

After the sin, the "eyes of both were opened, and they knew that they were naked; and they sewed fig leaves together and made themselves aprons." The nakedness factor invites our attention, but we shall pursue the matter more at length elsewhere. The text describes how they now feared God: "And they heard the sound of the Lord

God walking in the garden in the cool of the day, and the man and his wife hid themselves from the presence of the Lord God among the trees of the garden." God will drive home to them that they had done wrong by disobeying, but He would also promise them a Redeemer.

THE GRAVITY OF THE SIN

The punishment which God inflicts on Adam and Eve is a measure of the gravity of their offense. The *Catechism of the Catholic Church* emphasizes the point:

> 387.   Only the light of divine Revelation clarifies the reality of sin and particularly of the sin committed at mankind's origins. Without the knowledge Revelation gives of God we cannot recognize sin clearly and are tempted to explain it as merely a developmental flaw, a psychological weakness, a mistake, or the necessary consequence of an inadequate social structure, etc. Only in the knowledge of God's plan for man can we grasp that sin is an abuse of the freedom that God gives to created persons so that they are capable of loving him and loving one another.

The great lesson we should learn from the sin of Adam and Eve is that God loves us, that He will help us to rise from the sins we commit, and that Christ is our Redeemer.

Chapter 6

AFTER THE SIN

But the Lord God called to the man, and said to him, "Where are you?" And he said, "I heard the sound of thee in the garden, and I was afraid, because I was naked; and I hid myself." He said, "Who told you that you were naked? Have you eaten of the tree of which I commanded you not to eat?"

Note the shift to a reverse order in the appearances of the dramatis personae: for the sin, the serpent appears first, then the woman, finally the man. For the confession, God calls the man first, then the woman, finally the serpent. For the penance, the serpent gets it first, then the woman, finally the man.

Repentance is not all that difficult when the Lord God, who is already the Good Shepherd, the Good Samaritan, the Father of the Prodigal, smoothes the pathway for Adam and Eve to recognize their sin, to repent, and to resolve to sin no more. The magnanimity of God shows through when He looks past the excuses of Adam and Eve and recognizes their actual confession which they blurted out at the end of their excuses. The Lord God hears them out.

The man said, "The woman whom thou gavest to be with me, she gave me fruit of the tree, and I ate." Then the Lord God said to the woman, "What is this that you have done?" The woman said, "The serpent beguiled me, and I ate."

PUNISHMENT OF THE SERPENT

God vents His anger on the serpent with a raw curse: "On your belly shall you crawl." That punishment is obviously symbolic. Serpents did not have legs to walk on before this. The other punishment of the serpent is the great protoevangelium, an oracle about cosmic and mortal warfare to be fought to the death, with no quarters given on either side: "I will put enmity between you and the woman, and between your seed and her seed; he shall bruise your head and you shall bruise his heel." Let the serpent beware of that woman's implacable enmity; let it also know that its head will be crushed under the heel it is biting.

One may ask why this prophesy about the determined woman and her valiant offspring is in the Genesis story, but not, so far as I am aware, in creation myths of hunter-gatherers. The response may well be that the creation narrative which God kept alive among the ancestors of the Israelites constantly looked forward to the Incarnation, and therefore kept this mysterious saying intact. Whereas hunter-gatherers forgot this detail. They can now learn and accept the good news of Christ's coming from the Church.

That prophesy will henceforth become a link connecting epochs of the Chosen People. Noah will become the patriarch of a new people. Abraham will become the father of many nations of believers. Jacob will pick up thread of the prophesy: "The scepter shall not depart from Judah...until he comes to whom it belongs (Gen 49:10). Balaam will see a vision: "I see him, but not now; I behold him, but not nigh" Num 24:17). Promises are made to Moses, to David; Isaiah will see a glimpse of the virgin who will bear the

"God with us." Solomon will see a vision:

> And when peaceful stillness compassed everything
> and the night in its swift course was half spent,
> Your all-powerful word from heaven's royal throne
> bounded, a fierce warrior, into the doomed land,
> bearing the sharp sword of your inexorable de-
> cree...
>
> He reached to heaven, while he stood upon the earth.
> For all creation, in its several kinds, was being made
> anew... (Wis 18:14-16; 19:6; trans. of ICEL).

Luke will sound the trumpet to draw aside the curtain and stage the cosmic event itself: "Do not be afraid, Mary, for you have found favor with God. And behold, you will conceive in your womb and bear a son, and you shall call his name Jesus" (1:30-31). John will report the climax with the words:

> "Woman, behold your son." Then later: "It is fin-
> ished;" and he bowed his head and gave up his
> spirit.

But the enmity foretold in Genesis does not stop there. Though its head is bruised, the serpent continues to battle relentlessly: "Then the dragon was angry with the woman, and went off to make war on the rest of her offspring, on those who keep the commandments of God and bear testimony to Jesus" (Rev 12:13). That battle will continue until the end of time:

> Then comes the end, when he delivers the king-
> dom to God the Father, after destroying every rule

and every authority and power...When all things are subjected to him, then the Son himself will also be subjected to him who put all things under him, that God may be everything to everyone (1 Cor 15:24,28).

PUNISHMENT OF THE WOMAN

To the woman the Lord God announced two punishments: pain in childbearing, and subjection to her husband:

> To the woman he said, "I will greatly multiply your pain in childbearing; in pain you shall bring forth children, yet your desire shall be for your husband, and he shall rule over you."

As to the first penalty, Pope Pius XII taught that the Scripture did not state in what precise manner God considered this punishment nor how He would carry it out. Some claim, he continues, that before the sin childbirth was entirely painless, but that has not been proven. Nor is there any obligation, he said, that prevents women from seeking to make childbirth as painless as possible. This passage of the Bible does not forbid human intervention:

> In punishing Eve, God did not wish to forbid and did not forbid mothers to make use of means which render childbirth easier and less painful. One must not look for loopholes in the words of Scripture; these words remain true in the sense intended and expressed by the Creator, namely motherhood will give the mother much to endure. In what precise manner did God conceive this chastisement and how will He carry it out? Scripture does not

say (see address of Jan. 8, 1956; *The Pope Speaks* III, pp. 32-33).

Pius XII here declared that the passage: "In pain shall you bring forth children" is not to be taken literally as a command given to women to suffer pain during childbirth. We must understand the meaning of this passage of Scripture in its context he continued:

> In Genesis 3, 16 we read: "<u>In dolore paries filios</u>" ("In pain shall you bring forth children"). In order to understand this saying correctly, it is necessary to consider the condemnation declared by God in the whole of its context. In inflicting this punishment on our first parents and their descendants, God did not wish to forbid and did not forbid men to seek after and make use of all the riches of creation; to make progress step by step in culture; to make life in this world more bearable and more beautiful; to lighten the burden of fatigue, pain, sickness, and death; in a word, to subdue the earth (Gen. 1:28).

Thus the great moral theologian Pope Pius XII has nailed into a coffin a literal translation of the command that women must bear children in pain.

And Pope John Paul II nailed into another coffin a too literal translation of the other punishment given to Eve and her offspring: "Your husband...shall rule over you." Even in our day some good Catholic publications carry the message that the sentence must be taken literally, that wives take on an obligation of obedience to husbands at marriage, which is somewhat similar to a religious vow of obedience, which is a new element over and above the obligations and dynamics of mutual relations intrinsic and natural to the marriage relationship. The subjection is not one-sided but mutual, concludes the Pope. The passage responds to the usual difficulties raised, and is therefore quoted at length:

> *"Husbands, love your wives,"* love them because of that special and unique bond whereby in marriage a man a woman become "one flesh" (Gen 2:-24; Eph 5:31). In this love there is a fundamental *affirmation of the woman as a person*. This affirmation makes it possible for the female personality to develop fully and be enriched. This is precisely the way Christ acts as the bridegroom of the Church; he desires that she be "in splendor, without spot or wrinkle" (Eph 5:27). One can say this fully captures the whole "style" of Christ in dealing with women. Husbands should make their own the elements of this style in regard to their wives; analogously, all men should do the same in regard to women in every situation. In this way both men and women bring about "the sincere gift of self."

There is a difference, however, in the manner of the obedience of the Church to Christ, and the manner of obedience of a wife to her husband:

> The author of the Letter to the Ephesians sees no contradiction between an exhortation formulated in this way and the words: "Wives, be subject to your husbands, as to the Lord. For the husband is head of the wife" (5:22-23)). The author knows that this way of speaking, so profoundly rooted in the customs and the religious traditions of the

time, is to be understood and carried out in a new way: as a *"mutual subjection out of reverence for Christ"* (cf. Eph 5:21). This is especially true because the husband is called the "head" of the wife *as* Christ is the head of the Church; he is so in order to give "himself up for her" (Eph 5:25), and giving himself up for her means giving up even his own life. However, whereas in the relationship between Christ and the Church the subjection is only on the part of the Church, in the relationship between husband and wife the "subjection" is not one-sided but mutual (Apostolic Letter on the Dignity and Vocation of Women" 15 August 1988).

In brief, there is no innovation in Genesis 3:16 which obligates wives to obey their husbands in a manner which is different from, and over and above, natural dynamics of the marital relationship. Admittedly, birth pangs suffered by women, as well as difficulties of the marital relationship, may in reality be aggravated by the sinful condition of mankind. Whether the sacred author had this in mind here may be doubtful. Rather, he uses well-known human sufferings as a symbol to help us reflect how great is God's displeasure with sin. What he presents symbolically, we need not, indeed we ought not, interpret literally. When he brings to mind human pains to motivate us against sin, we ought to be teachable to his method. We do him an injustice if we imagine that he thereby registers a real change in the natural world because of original sin.

PUNISHMENT OF THE MAN

Finally the Lord God turns to Adam who had allowed Eve to seduce him:

Because you have listened to the voice of your wife, and have eaten of the tree of which I commanded you, "You shall not eat of it," cursed is the ground because of you; in toil you shall eat of it all the days of your life; thorns and thistles it shall bring forth to you; and you shall eat the plants of the field. In the sweat of your face you shall eat bread till you return to the ground, for out of it you were taken; you are dust and to dust you shall return.

We note that the curse on the ground is lifted by God in Genesis 8:21, when He was pleased with the sacrifice made by Noah: "And when the Lord smelled the pleasing odor, the Lord said in his heart, "I will never again curse the ground because of man..."

Again, we need not interpret the words spoken to Adam literally in the meaning that God caused a change in the natural world because of original sin. The relaxed manner in which Pious XII and John Paul II interpret the punishments inflicted on the woman, may also be applied to the punishment of the man. The sacred author is employing hardships experienced because of the limitations of nature as rhetorical symbols to impart to us a picture of the Lord God's righteous and intense displeasure with sin. The author may also imply that man makes life unnecessarily harder for himself by committing sin. Nature appears to be hostile only when man casts off intimate and friendly relations with his Creator.

If we suppose that nothing natural was changed in this world by original sin, how then shall we understand the passage of Paul to the Romans:

For creation was subjected to futility, not of its own will but by the will of him who subjected it in hope; because the creation itself will be set free from its bondage to decay and obtain the glorious liberty of the children of God. We know that the whole creation has been groaning in travail together until now, and not only the creation, but we ourselves who have been the first fruits of the Spirit groan inwardly as we wait for the adoption as sons, the redemption of our bodies (8:20-23).

The passage has poetic resonance, ascribing to inanimate nature feelings and aspirations similar to those of man. Obviously inanimate nature does not really "groan." Poetry must be interpreted as poetry, lacking literal precisions.

Moreover, Paul has in mind the above passage of Genesis 3:17-19, and 5:19, namely the curse of God on the earth because of Adam's transgression (cf. Joseph A. Fitzmyer, *Romans*, Doubleday, N.Y., 1993, p. 505). If the parent passage to which Paul refers is already symbolic, Paul's passage referring back to it is to be read in like manner. Waters flowing downriver never rise above the headwaters of the source. Romans 8:20-23 is not only poetic, it builds this poetry upon the foundation of symbolism in Genesis. Poetry built upon symbolism does not thereby become a new dogma to be interpreted in a literal sense. This passage of Romans does not teach that an actual change came into the cosmos with Adam's sin. What it does is to make this glance back into the garden of Eden to reflect light forward to shine upon upon our pathway leading toward the escatological glories yet to come.

EXPULSION

Genesis 3 next recounts how the man called his wife's name Eve, which in Hebrew sounds like the word for "living." He does so because she was the mother of all the living. Perhaps the sacred author intends thereby to show their reconciliation with each other. It is a beautiful name, an honor, a recognition of her dignity. The man takes up again the romance he began when he had called her *Ishsha* "because she was taken taken out of the Man" (Gen 2:-23). He courts her once more with the new name *Eva* "because she was the mother of all living" (Gen 3:20). The action implies that they resumed marital relationships by means of which she becomes the mother of all mankind.

This short passage about a new name appears to be a break in the flow of the narrative. The sacred author might more logically have skipped it to continue the story. Shall we attribute to the human author a digression to allow a tribute to motherhood? Perhaps the sacred author thought of his own mother here - for undoubtedly he had a mother. Perhaps he thought also of his wife and her care for his children. And so perhaps the author used this opportunity to give a salute of honor to motherhood in the Book of Genesis which would be read for all ages to come. And the Holy Spirit did not object to allowing a short pause in the narrative, to provide this recognition, this accolade, this salute to womanhood and to motherhood. I say, perhaps.

The Lord God next makes for Adam and his wife garments of skin, and clothes them therewith. The sacred author takes care to not extinguish hope: God loves them still and anew, even though He must sentence them severely to live in altered circumstances, definitely inferior to their experience before sin. He kindly makes for them a sturdy set of clothes. Even more, He gives them a hand when they dress themselves in clothes for the first time. Having shown them this sign of affection, He then passes the sentence as He must.

Note the succession of concepts: naked without shame before the sin -> naked with shame after the sin -> clothed with animal skins when they left the garden. If naked without shame symbolizes innocence and obedience, and naked with shame then symbolizes lost innocence and a state of disobedience, what then does their sturdy animal clothing symbolize? Do we see in it a symbol of a more experienced Adam and Eve, street-wise now against further machinations of the serpent, with better protection than before the experience of the sin? And by illustrating the experience of the first parents, does the sacred author warn us against being naive in this wicked world? For in it "Your adversary, the devil prowls around like a roaring lion, seeking some one to devour" (1 Peter 5:8).

There may be more in the symbol of sturdy clothes for use outside of the garden: clothing allows us to hide our inner secrets when going about in public view. Besides parading exaggerated pretensions about ourselves, or hiding talents from public exposure, clothing also allows us to engage in daily public converse without revealing our inner thoughts. We can hide in privacy our devout innocence and virtuous obedience to God without parading it before the public. Our naked interior we can hide from public view, also if it is virtuous. Sometimes, in the public forum outside of the garden of Eden, it is expedient to hide our virtue from prying eyes and from enemies. The sacred writer symbolizes the fact that God wants us to be "wise as serpents and simple as doves" when we cope with life outside of the garden where all is is not innocence, all is not holy, nor can all be trusted.

In consequence of their sin Adam and Eve must now leave the garden. The sin was grave, as the sentence indicates. Readers, beware! implies the sacred author. The two must leave God's private garden, depart from His gracious presence, and exit into the secular world. As they slump out of the gate, the Lord clanks down the bars behind them, cuts off access to the tree of life, and leaves them much to their own devices. No longer will they walk with the Lord God on wooded paths during the cool of the evening breeze. So does the sacred author dramatize God's "tough love," to dissuade Adam and Eve from ever sinning again, and to deter us from the same.

> Then the Lord God said, "Behold, the man has become like one of us, knowing good and evil; and now, lest he put forth his hand and take also of the tree of life, and eat, and live forever" -- therefore the Lord God sent him forth from the garden of Eden, to till the ground from which he was taken. He drove out the man; and at the east of the garden of Eden he placed the cherubim, and a flaming sword which turned every way, to guard the way to the tree of life.

Adam, now outside of the garden, will once again till the ground from which he was taken. God had previously transferred him into the garden from outside. While in the state of grace he could live on intimate terms with God. By his mortal sin Adam had lost the gift of intimacy with God.

Now he lived once more outside of the garden, separated from God's presence. The symbolic action dramatizes the tremendous evil of sin.

Chapter 7

IMMUNITY FROM BODILY DEATH

When the Fathers of the Council of Trent met in 1546 to clarify teachings on original sin, Cardinal del Monte, one of the three Papal Legates, proposed that they first of all study the work which had been done in this area in times past. They are to build on these teachings, and ought not debate speculatively about scholastic disputations. They should therefore collect and examine the decrees which the Church had accepted and approved at general and provincial councils (cf. *Concilium Tridentinum*, Angelus Massarellus, Vol. I, p. 166). Massarellus conducted the official protocol which provides us with priceless data about the deliberations.

Political realities had blocked efforts for several decades to assemble a general council of the Church for the purpose of responding to questions generated by the Protestant Reformation. Finally in November 1544 Pope Paul III (1534-1549) called the Fathers to Trent for the 19th General Council of the Church. Trent was a German city to the north of Italy on the road to Innsbruck, a great road which for over a thousand years had carried traffic between Rome and Germany. The Council was solemnly opened there on December 13, 1545, by the three Papal Legates, with thirty one bishops in attendance and forty-eight theologians and canonists and technical experts to assist them (Philip Hughes, *The Church in Crisis* 348).

The participants, assisted by theologians, set up procedures as follows: only bishops and generals of religious orders should have the right to vote, but not the designated theologians. When the designated theologians held an official debate in the presence of the Fathers, such a meeting was named a "particular congregation." When the Council members met to discuss the matter under the presidency of the Legates, this was called a "general congregation." A final and public meeting to vote on and then promulgate declarations and definitions was called a "session." Twenty five public sessions were held between 1545 and 1563, the year of the final closing (cf. Hughes op. cit., 350). The session on original sin which we study here is number five, completed on June 17, 1546.

By May of 1946 four public sessions had already taken place and procedures were well grooved. On the second of May, 1546, the three Papal Legates received their instructions from Pope Paul III to proceed with Session Five, on original sin and some disciplinary matters.

Political tensions abounded, threatening to interrupt the proceedings. To avoid needless confrontation the Council employed subterfuges. For example, the designated theologians might be asked to conduct unofficial preliminary debates among themselves outside the Council, in a separate building. They contributed to the Council's work, without raising a red flag to aggravate the Emperor. But after this warm-up, they could then present their focussed views at the Council itself.

The Legates, highly capable, were Cardinal Cervini (the future Pope Marcellus II, 1555); Cardinal Del Monte (the future Julius III, 1549-1555); and Cardinal Pole. A good account of the proceedings is given in Hubert Jedin's *A History of the Council of Trent*. Also available is a copy of the official protocol and notes in *Concilium Tridentinum*

(CT) written by Massarellus, secretary of the Council.

The Legates initiated deliberations on original sin by announcing the topic at a general congregation on May 21. The first unofficial debate by theologians was scheduled for May 24. The Legates presented to the designated theologians guideline topics or questions to begin deliberations (CT V, 163-164; I, p. 439). Their content is as follows:

1. What evidence from Holy Scripture and Apostolic Tradition have the Fathers and the Holy See employed against opponents of original sin?   What principles are involved, and who are concerned with the problem?

2. Following the precedent of the ancient councils, the difference between original sin and other sins should be formulated not in terms of a definition of its nature, but on the basis of a description and of consequences.

3. How is a person freed from original sin? When the sin is remitted, is the remission complete, or do effects (traces, remnants) remain? If the latter, what effectiveness do they retain? (Cf. also Jedin II,134).

The Legates deliberately issued these guidelines to prevent the Council from becoming bogged down in disputations by partisans of scholastic theories. They put a tight rein on members to adhere resolutely to what can be found in Scripture and Tradition. A less disciplined approach risked igniting the explosive tinder of theological tensions between Seculars, Dominicans, Franciscans, Conventuals, Augustinians, Carmelites, Servites, and Benedictines - all with axes to grind about the nature of original sin. Thus begun auspiciously, discussions progressed rapidly. The thirty designated theologians addressed themselves to the above questions at meetings held on May 24 and 25. The Legates, notes Massarellus (CT V 164), praised them greatly for their contributions (maximopere laudati sunt).

Because the discussion by the theologians was not an official part of the Council proceedings, no protocol was recorded. A very sketchy summary of the responses recorded by Massarellus (CT V,164-166) indicates the following contents: original sin is derived from the originating sin of Adam, is spread not through imitation but through propagation, exists in each person, and differs from other sins insofar as it is not contracted through an act of the will by individuals; its guilt and penalty are remitted through Baptism. The principle effects are temporal and eternal death, concupiscence exceeding the limits of reason, an inclination of the will to evil, ignorance, infirmity, loss of grace, and hatred by God (CT V,164-166). Note that the theologians explicitly declared that "temporal death," which means physical death, is a result of original sin. This will be challenged before the final definition is formulated.

CANON I OF CARTHAGE SIDELINED

The Legates observed with disapproval that the theologians had not provided much documentation from Scripture and Tradition. At the May 28 session the Legates therefore mandated a public reading of pertinent Pontifical and Conciliar documents which they had assembled for this purpose. After the reading, they presented the documents to all the Fathers of the Council for further study (CT I, 439; V, 169-172; Cf. Jedin II,142).

Conspicuously missing from the documents is canon 1 of Carthage 418, the one so dear to St. Augustine. Canon 2 of Carthage 418 is cited, and Carthage 418 is mentioned by name as having issued it (cf. CT V, 170). This fact makes the omission of the famous Canon 1 of Carthage 418 all the more remarkable. That Canon 1 had declared that Adam would not have died physically had he not sinned. Carthage had made it a priority declaration, and St. Augustine had used it as a prime weapon against Pelagius. But the Papal Legates apparently did not circulate it at Trent. It reads as follows:

> All the bishops established in the sacred synod of the Carthaginian Church have decided that whoever says that Adam, the first man, was made mortal, so that, whether he sinned or whether he did not sin, he would die in body, that is he would go out of the body not because of the merit of sin but by reason of nature, let him be <u>anathema.</u>

Although that canon was excluded, specific parts of canon 2 of Carthage (418), and canon 2 of Orange (529) were read at the general congregation on 28 May 1946. Massarellus, in the protocol (CT V, 171), placed parentheses around that part of the Orange text which refers to <u>physical death</u>. The battle was now engaged. Evidently there would be controversy about that part, and the protocol gave it special treatment by enclosing in parenthesis the term "death...of the body." By the tactic of the parenthesis the Legates put the Fathers on special alert to ponder about <u>physical death</u>, whether it is connected with original sin.

DISCUSSION: WHY IS IMMORTALITY
NOT RESTORED AT BAPTISM?

A general congregation followed on May 31. Among the forty-six Fathers who either made interventions or gave their opinions about the contents of part one, only one mentions the subject of physical death. The Superior General of the Servites asserted that physical death (mors temporalis) is a punishment for original sin (CT V, 176). When discussing part two, also only one mentioned ejection from paradise and death as punishment for the sin. No discussion about this is noted.

In the summary of the total deliberations, Massarellus states that the Fathers had responded to part one by inferring that God punished Adam for his sin by inflicting "the kind of death with which God had threatened him." That takes the heat off the Council. With such a wording the Council could avoid explicit mention of physical death, and allow the Scriptures and Tradition to speak for themselves. Massarellus records in the protocol that many speakers had asked the Legates to compose the decrees in accord with earlier decisions of councils.

After celebrating the Feast of the Ascension on June 3, a general congregation followed on Friday, June 4, to continue discussion on part two of the propositions. Due to the summer heat sessions would henceforth be reduced to a duration of three hours (CT V, 185). Physical death now finally came up for discussion. A delegate declared that four effects of original sin are listed in a well known document: 1) it closes the doors of heaven to the person; 2) brings eternal damnation; 3) makes the person impotent to resist vice, and 4) subjects the person to temporal death.

Baptism, he commented, removes the first three effects. But it does not remove the fourth effect, namely physical death. However that effect will also be removed finally, when the last enemy of all will be destroyed (cf. 1 Cor 15:26: "The last enemy to be destroyed is death").

Why does Baptism not immediately free us from physical death by the merits of the grace of Christ? continued the speaker. St. Augustine, he said, answers this in *The City of God* 13:4. If Baptism were to free us from our mortality, our faith could not be not be what it must be. For faith must be based on the hope of things unseen. If Baptism would make us suddenly immortal, faith would vanish because of the dramatic results which we could see with our eyes (CT V, 191). That is, if everybody who is baptized at the font would walk away with an immortal body, such an effect would be so notorious as to become an obstacle to freely given faith. There is no record in the protocol indicating that anyone agreed or disagreed.

Discussion, centering mostly on concupiscence, continued through June 5. In his summary of the two day discussion Massarellus says nothing about physical death, except for the statement made that the death of Christ frees us from the power of Satan, from the powers of hell, from death, from weaknesses, and that it effects a total remission of sins (CT V, 195). "Death" is not specified further, whether it be physical or spiritual.

On June 6 Massarellus leaked a preview of the coming draft to three influential Fathers, and to two Franciscan and two Dominican theologians. On June 7 the three Papal Legates submitted this Draft One, which they had composed, to the Council members (CT I, 439; V, 196-197). The

Papal Legates reserved the right to present proposals, which the members could then debate. Draft One, read and examined at a general congregation on June 8, had four canons; we confine our attention to the subject of death in the draft of canons 1 and 2.

> Canon 1. If anyone does not profess that Adam ... truly incurred the wrath and indignation of God (from which death followed), with which God had previously threatened him [brackets in text]... (CT V, p. 196).

> Canon 2. If anyone asserts...that he incurred because of this sin of disobedience only death and penalties of the body...but not the sin, <u>anathema sit.</u>

The protocol presents a number of alternative drafts and formulas, in two of which death of the body as well as of the soul is mentioned (CT V, p. 198). The Fathers now had to choose. On Tuesday June 8, after a preliminary reading of the draft proposed by the Legates, discussions followed on that day, and were continued on the next morning. In the summary of the interventions Massarellus reveals a significant development: many of the Fathers had requested that "death of the soul" be substituted for "death of body and soul": "*Cui pro poena debetur utraque mors* etc., multi petierunt dici *quod mors est animae* (italics his, CT V,208). By this sentence in the protocol Massarellus makes it clear that "many" of the Fathers asked that "death of the body" as punishment for original sin be excluded from the definition. Their intervention prevailed. This sentence indicates that the Council of Trent knowingly avoided a definition which would teach that death of the body is a punishment for original sin.

Pressed for time, a general congregation was held on June 14, the Monday after Pentecost. Cardinal Del Monte apologized for calling the meeting on the holiday, as time was short. He asked Massarellus to read the amended draft which took into account the recent discussions. New amendments, those made since June 8, were set off clearly. Canon 2 was now amended to read "death of the soul," instead of "death of body and soul" (CT V,218).

Trent's canon 2, using part of a canon of Orange II (529), casually mentions death of the body as a common belief. Then by astute wording the Council avoids defining explicitly that physical death is a punishment for original sin. Trent allowed the popular belief to remain in place, though without taking a stand on the question.

The Fathers, who had heard the previous discussions that physical death was one of the punishments of original sin, were certainly aware that it was a belief hallowed by the authority of Saint Augustine, prevalent in scholastic theology, and that it was a persuasion held dear by Christians. Perhaps believers are inclined to hesitate to attribute to God an original plan that includes physical death for humans, even if original sin had not been committed. Trent worded the definition discreetly to avoid offending pious ears, but did not make this popular belief into a part of the definition to be held by the Church.

THE DECREE IS PROMULGATED, JUNE 17, 1546

The finally amended draft was read to the Assembly on the evening of June 16, at which time a preliminary vote was taken. Last minute maneuvers to obtain a definition of the Immaculate Conception failed. The date for the next session was set for July 29. The usual censure against those who were absent from the Council was approved. Cardinal del Monte asked all present to attend the great session of the next day. All was now ready for promulgation of the decrees on the following day, June 17, Thursday within the Octave of Pentecost. A weary secretary Massarellus signed his protocol with the remark: "Dimittitur congregatio hora prima noctis." I think it means that they closed the meeting at 1:00 AM in the wee hours of June 17. The Communion Fast from food and drink had presumably begun at midnight. Shed a tear of thanks for the gallant Fathers of Trent.

The 4 Cardinals, 9 Archbishops, 49 Bishops, 2 Abbots, 3 Superiors General (Jedin II,161; cf. CT I, 439) gathered on morning of June 17 for public Session V of the Council of Trent to promulgate the Decree on Original Sin, and regulations about reading of Holy Scripture and preaching. The Session began with the celebration of a Solemn High Mass in honor of the Holy Spirit. The celebrant was Bishop Allesandro Piccolomini, and the preacher was Marcus Laureus, O.P., whose sermon was "more remarkable for ingenuity than depth of thought" (Jedin II,161). He spoke loftily about the Church as the Paradise of the virtues and gifts of the Holy Spirit.

After Mass the vote was taken. The vote on the main decrees on original sin was positive and near unanimous. It is now a doctrine of the Church. The two canons which concern us read as follows:

Trent, Canon 1: If anyone does not profess that Adam, the first man, by transgressing God's commandment in paradise, at once lost the holiness and justice in which he had been constituted; and that, offending God by his sin, he drew upon himself the wrath and indignation of God and consequently death with which God had threatened him, and together with death captivity in the power of him who henceforth "has the power of death" (Heb. 2:14) i.e., the devil; and that "the whole Adam, body and soul, was changed for the worse through the offence of his sin" anathema sit (DS 1511; Dupuis 508).

Trent, Canon 2: If anyone asserts that Adam's sin harmed only him and not his descendants and that the holiness and justice received from God which he lost was lost only for him and not for us also; or that, stained by the sin of disobedience, he transmitted to all mankind only death and the sufferings of the body but not sin as well which is the death of the soul, anathema sit...(DS 1512; Dupuis 509).

THE CATECHISM ON PHYSICAL DEATH

Today the Church goes one step further than Trent by the teaching in *CCC* 1008 and again in 1018 that physical death was brought about by original sin:

As a consequence of original sin, man must suffer "bodily death, from which man would have been immune had he not sinned" (*CCC 1018, cf.GS #18*).

The *CCC* is "a sure norm for teaching the faith and thus a valid and legitimate instrument for ecclesial communion...This catechism is given to (the Church's pastors and the Christian faithful) that it may be a sure and authentic reference text for teaching doctrine and particularly for preparing local catechisms" (Apostolic Constitution on the publication of the Catechism of the Catholic Church, John Paul II, October 11, 1992).

Despite the refusal of the Council of Trent to define the doctrine that Adam would have been immune from physical death if he had not sinned, the Church today proclaims it as part of its catechesis. Actually, Trent did not oppose the common belief, and only refused to make it binding once and for all.

The *CCC*'s inclusion of the doctrine is of great teaching value to dramatically emphasize the evil of sin, of disobedience to God. Death follows sin, so beware! Genesis certainly does the same by pairing death with sin. This is an excellent teaching aid, already begun in Genesis, now continued in our Catechism.

There may be theological reasons of great depth in the teaching that bodily death is a consequence of original sin, aspects of a truth which remain to be mined and discovered. Sin is moral corruption of the sinner's soul, and corruption of the body through death may be mystically associated with sin in the eyes of God as well as of man. On the other hand, as we shall see in the chapter "Christ, Pantokrator," suffering and death, though confontational against our natural feelings, become our supreme accomplishment, honor and ornament when we accept them with the power of Christ (see Matthias Scheeben, 424).

The same theologian attributes to Adam a lesser existential value if he had not suffered and died. He writes:

> In this respect, too, the order of grace established by Christ is more wonderful and splendid than that of the first Adam. As Adam had not merited grace, so he was not to have purchased the state of glory by suffering and death. God exacted of him no true sacrifice as the price of glory. Although the painless manifestation of tender love for God could avail as merit for glory, still for Adam heaven was given rather than bought, since it cost him nothing. The new Adam (Christ), on the contrary, has purchased grace itself for us by a true sacrifice; and although we do not recover integrity through Him along with grace, yet we are summoned to battle and sacrifice in order to storm heaven and thus win it. Are not this battle and this sacrifice more noble, more glorious, more sublime than the tranquil state enjoyed by Adam, seeing that he received his happy life entirely from the goodness of His Creator, without meriting it by a worthy return of service in the immolation of himself? (455).

Are we puzzled by the fact that our present cosmos is not designed for human life which is immune from physical death? One response to the puzzle can be that God already foresaw that Adam would commit original sin, hence there was no need for God to design the cosmos for a condition which would never become real. I confess that this solution, although proposed by some people, does not please me.

Other considerations remain to be solved. We note that the

CCC does not state that Adam was already immune from physical death before he sinned. Nor does it teach that he enjoyed perpetual youth and freedom from various natural hardships during his life before sin. Many things remain unsaid and unresolved, if man's natural condition of dying a biological death began only after original sin.

A number of reasons converge to indicate that man's immunity from bodily death, as taught in GS 18 and the *CCC*, has the fuller meaning of eternal death of body and soul. The context of GS 18 is about man's yearning for eternal life, not for mere biological continuity on earth. Furthermore, footnotes 14 and 15 of GS 18 refer to biblical texts that pertain to spiritual death invoked by evil deeds; they do not treat about biological death. Finally, the Council of Trent yolked together death from original sin and captivity under the power of the devil. But saints who die a bodily death in holiness are not captives of the devil. GS 18 and CCC 1008 therefore point more plausibly to eternal death than to temporal biological death. If that is correct, then neither Genesis, nor the rest of the Bible, nor Trent, nor Vatican II, nor the *Catechism of the Catholic Church* indicates with certainty that man was ever immune from natural biological death before original sin. However, I remain open for correction on this point.

I hope that the Church will concern herself with this question out of pastoral regard for the people. If we can accept death humbly from God as the natural term of our life on earth, we are at peace with Him. Whereas if we suspect that it is a punishment inflicted on us intrusively for the sin of Adam and Eve, we may die puzzled and less peacefully. A more elucidated doctrine about death would also fortify us in the battle against euthanasia.

Chapter 8

TRENT ON CONCUPISCENCE

The Fathers of the Council of the Council of Trent, in 1546, asserted that the existence of concupiscence in ourselves leaves our free will intact, that the attraction to sin is not sin, nor is it displeasing to God. Though it remains after Baptism, it harms none who cope with it dutifully.

During the sometimes acrimonious debate the turbid concept of the attraction toward sin which remains in us after Baptism became an object of special attention. The view that our wills are now almost impotent was tested. A speaker suggested that concupiscence in us is so evil that we can never be perfectly justified while we live on this earth in our flesh. Only when we finally slough off the vile body at the time of death can we really be clean internally. But that pessimistic view of our fallen nature did not gather much support among the assembled Fathers. In the end they gave a far more positive evaluation of our present condition during the time of testing in this mortal life.

Agreement was near unanimous when the final vote was taken: Baptism forgives original sin, and eradicates it from the soul. Baptism effectuates the "putting off the old person and putting on the new, created after the likeness of God, innocent, unstained, pure and guiltless." The sacrament renews those who are cleansed into becoming "beloved children of God, heirs of God and fellow heirs with Christ, so that nothing henceforth holds them back from entering into heaven" (DS 1515, Dupuis 512). The Fathers thus vindicated the spiritual integrity of those who are cleansed of original sin by Baptism. But they acknowledged that we remain subject to inclinations to sin after Baptism.

The main thrust of the final resolution is a confirmation that our wills are indeed free. This cleared the ground for canon 5 of the subsequent Session on Justification held six months later. It reads: "If anyone says that after Adam's sin the free will of man is lost and extinct, or that it is an empty concept, a term without real foundation, indeed a fiction introduced by Satan into the Church, anathema sit" (DS 1555; Dupuis 1955).

Anabaptists were denying Baptism to infants at the time. In response Trent reiterated the tradition that infants are to be baptized for the remission of sins. Trent thus confirmed once more the Apostolic Tradition of infant Baptism.

Catholic Theologian Pighius had proposed that descendants of Adam do not inherit original sin in reality, but only in name. It covers humanity in globo. The Fathers responded sharply that the sin of Adam is indeed a reality in each person individually. Baptism therefore heals us internally by washing away this sin. The sacrament is not an insignificant external formality, a mere legal device entitling people to enter the Church.

THEOLOGIAN PRESENTS PESSIMISTIC VIEWPOINT

On May 24-25 the designated theologians of the Council conducted discussions apropos to our subject, of which no protocol was kept. A good record remains, however, of the contribution of one of the theologians, the Spanish secular priest Juan Morilla. He was the designated theologian for

Cardinal Pole and commanded a powerful position. By our good fortune he adhered to a text which had been prepared beforehand of which a record survives. It lifts the curtain to reveal the remarkable position which he presented there.

Morilla began with a presentation of proof from Holy Scripture that the existence of original sin is an undisputed fact. He confirmed this with the witness of Councils which had opposed Pelagian errors. He then cited the Decree directed against the Jacobites which again proved that original sin is a part of the doctrine of the Church. In addition to these documents of the Magisterium he cited the systematic development of theology which confirms that original sin is the foundation for the teaching of the Church that sanctifying grace comes to us from Christ.

Theologian Morilla then moved into the area which more directly concerns the question of concupiscence, discussing whether it is a punishment for original sin. He championed the opinion that Adam's psychological condition was changed utterly for the worse because of original sin. His view is dramatic and extreme, bordering on the assumption that concupiscence corrupts human nature so completely that the free will can no longer assert itself against evil tendencies. Morilla allows that the will remains theoretically free, but practically is almost coerced by forces of concupiscence.

The theologian asserted that Adam, before the sin, had possessed an unspoiled human nature whose capabilities were rectified for him through the grace of God. As founder of the human race, and by reason of a covenant with God, it was possible for Adam to preserve these gifts intact for his descendants through obedience. But it was also possible for him to lose them for himself and for us through disobedience.

These primal gifts, continued Fr. Morilla, consisted in the integrity of nature and above all in the special grace of God (singularis gratia Dei). The gift also brought an inner harmony to the soul in which the power of reason ruled over the will and over the soul's lower faculties. Reason also had the power to rule over creation, enabling Adam to adjust external living conditions to happy advantage.

With the Fall, continued Morilla, evil concupiscence began to rule over humans, rendering them rebellious against God and enslaving them to sin. Concupiscence does not absolutely rule by coercion, but it does indeed generate a certain spontaneous necessity (necessitate quadam spontanea). The consequences of original sin are: physical death in this world, plus loss of the beatific vision in the next world which "almost all scholastic theologians hold," he asserted. Furthermore, the sin merits pains of sense, as Augustine taught, and such recent theologians as Gregory of Rimini and John Driedo hold. He was moving now into assertions which the Church has never taught.

The passing on of original sin to every offspring of Adam, continued the speaker, occurs by the following mechanism: the soul, which God creates good, becomes united with the body through propagation; that is, by sexual intercourse which is replete with concupiscence. It is in this manner that each person's soul becomes contaminated with original sin by way of propagation (Cf. Jedin II, 136-137).

What happens, then, when original sin is remitted through Baptism? The speaker asserted that through our incorporation into Christ by Baptism, the guilt of the sin and the punishment of eternal damnation are extinguished. We again become children of God thereby. Baptism, however, does not remove the concupiscence which is inherited with original sin, he continued, for this remains in the reborn as a moral task to be accomplished. Before Baptism this concupiscence is a part of the essence of original sin (in essentia peccati). We might call it a kind of matter of the sin. After Baptism it remains only as a left-over influence of original sin. It remains as a hindrance against doing good. It is able to prevent the perfection of justification in this life.

Concupiscence is therefore not sin in the strict sense of the word, but it is a gravitation in the baptized which pulls them downward toward sin. So far the contents of Fr. Morilla's intervention. His terms "imperfect justification" and "gravitation toward evil" would become cardinal issues of the debate. For the above see Jedin II, 136-137.

Martin Butzer was cited by another Father during the debate as having claimed that original sin is merely covered over by Baptism, not really taken away. This apparently electrified the Fathers who seized upon it as an expression of the essence of the opponents' teaching. It clarified the picture. The concept that Baptism spreads "whitewash" over original sin to hide it instead of washing the soul clean was condemned in the final definition.

A consensus began to gel among the thirty-four Fathers who spoke on June 4 and 5: concupiscence is not sin in the strict sense of the word. One disagreed, however. For

a full hour he proposed and promoted his novel explanation. Though others had to wait, the audience gave him
appreciative attention. He championed the idea, with a nod
to St. Paul's terminology, that concupiscence <u>was</u> <u>a</u> <u>sin</u>
only before Baptism. After Baptism it is no more than an
<u>occasion</u> <u>of</u> <u>sin</u>. In the end, however, this clever but sim-
plistic solution was not accepted.

Another went to the heart of the problem, asserting that
concupiscence is not a sin. It cannot be a sin. Because
what belongs to human nature itself cannot possibly be a
sin. This came nearer to the formula which the Council
finally accepted, but did not coincide with it completely.

The long intervention which had described concupiscence
as a sin before Baptism, and only an occasion of sin after
Baptism, did not sit well with the Augustinian Seripando.
He rose to make a powerful rejoinder in which he stressed
his belief in the immense evil of concupiscence. Seripando
admitted that after Baptism concupiscence can no longer
be called sin in the strict sense of that term. But it is and
remains in itself, in a certain sense (<u>aliqua</u> <u>ratione</u>), something which is sinful because it is a punishment for sin. It
is also the root and cause of many actual sins.

Seripando now came to the flashpoint: concupiscence
itself must be something sinful by reason of its very existence in us. For it is nothing less than a hindrance against
the perfect fulfillment of the will of God. As long as a
person is not free from it, even from its unconscious influence, a person is unable to fulfill God's commandment:
"Thou shalt not covet." This command forbids not only
voluntary lust, but, in accordance with the teaching of St.
Augustine, also the spontaneous movements of lust which

the will rejects. Not until one is dead can this be sloughed off, and only then can the perfect inner justification be realized. Concupiscence is therefore a weakness (infirmitas) in humans, and it is a moral task. It forces humans to engage their full strength in the battle against evil. This powerfully spurs the justified to feel the need of grace and preserves them from self-righteousness.

When the speaker sat down after this climactic rhetoric, a colleague asked bluntly whether he is not in Luther's camp with this concept. To which Seripando replied that he is not. Although he says that concupiscence displeases God, he does not say that concupiscence condemns one to hell. That is because God forgives its guilt. Even children who die without Baptism are freed from condemnation in one manner or other. [N.B. He softens here the stern theology of Morilla who would condemn the unbaptized to hell.] But the fact remains, so Seripando persisted, that concupiscence is in some manner opposed to God. For this reason preachers should not be forbidden to say that concupiscence remains in the baptized as a sin. That is what Paul says. That is what Augustine says. Preachers should be allowed to say it in so many words. This should not be forbidden. But they should then explain more exactly what they mean by that.

On the other hand, continued Seripando, preachers who want to deny that concupiscence is a sin ought to explain why they wish to deny it. Namely the fact that it's guilt is forgiven and so concupiscence does not condemn one to hell (cf. Jedin II, 146-147). The Seripando-Morillo contention that concupiscence is sin did not win the consent of the majority. They had trodden on sensitive toes. One of the speakers, who also called concupiscence a sin, stated that he is forced to choose his words carefully lest he be accused of leanings toward the Lutheran concept of its nature.

On June 7 the Legates distributed to all the Fathers a draft of a decree on original sin which they had composed. It consisted of four canons; canon 4 of the draft concerning concupiscence is apropos to our subject; it states that children are to be baptized to obtain eternal life. Baptism remits original sin and whatever is sin in the proper sense of the word. But "concupiscence" or a "tinder" remains, as "a weakness and sickness of nature." This is not sin in the proper sense of the word, though it is from sin and inclines to sin. Appealing to Augustine and Thomas, the draft proposes as not unacceptable the Thomistic formula according to which the _formal_ element of original sin is forgiven by Baptism, while the _material_ element (concupiscence) remains. That assessment of concupiscence, however, did not make its way into the final definition.

That draft was read at a general congregation on June 8. The Fathers discussed it during the week which followed. Is it not self-contradictory, some asked, to state that Baptism completely blots out original sin; to say that nothing remains in the soul after Baptism which could be offensive in the eyes of God; and then to turn around and state that relics of original sin remain in the soul? The question was posed but not answered. The records provide no evidence that anyone volunteered to articulate a better solution for this apparent dilemma. The final decree is so worded that it did not clarify the matter. Before we analyze the final definition concerning concupiscence, several related points deserve our attention.

HOLINESS AND JUSTICE vs. SANCTIFYING GRACE

A number spoke against the draft's wording that God initially endowed Adam with "holiness and justice." They preferred the terms "rectitude and innocence" (cf. John Endres, OP, 80). The hidden agenda in this may have been an attempt to becloud the concept that the initial gift to Adam was something above and beyond what man possesses by his nature. If Adam's initial gifts were natural only, then original sin would have damaged nature itself. But if the gifts were supernatural, they might be pealed off their natural base without damaging it. That is, the human intellect, will, and body might then remain intact after original sin just as before, without being weakened or deformed. The point is pivotal to the Council's doctrine that the will, a natural endowment, remains free after original sin. Opponents held that concupiscence arising from original sin deprives the will its native freedom. A determined majority opposed this. The words "holiness and justice" in the final definition signify its supernatural character. If supernatural, its deprivation need not harm nature iself, much as switching off a light does not damage the light bulb. That original sin did not distort, deform, or weaken man in the area of his natural endowments - his native powers of intellect and will - thus remains plausible.

Note that the definition does not employ the term "sanctifying grace" to identify Adam's supernatural gift. It uses a less precise term, namely "holiness and justice." Perhaps the Fathers did not wish to equate the grace of Adam before the Fall (grace of God) with the sanctifying grace which Christ bestows after the Fall (grace of Christ). Present at the Council were sharp theologians who might become trigger happy if they sensed that the honor of their

Religious Order came on the dock. A notorious and heated controversy between Scotists and Thomists smoldered below the urbane surface of Council proceedings. Scotists asserted that the grace of Adam before the Fall was already the grace of Christ. "Nonsense" would opposing Thomists say to that. They claimed that God, but not the Incarnate Christ, gave the first grace to Adam. For the Incarnation of Christ came into God's plans in consequence of Adam's sin. According to their opinion it would be absurd to assert that Christ gave grace to Adam before even Christ was born upon this earth. The Papal Legates walked a tight rope to prevent a semblance of taking sides in scholastic theological warfare. Members of the various Religious Orders present at the Council might take very seriously a perceived obligation to defend their Order's partisan honor.

Pope John Paul II, however, does not hesitate today to call the original grace of Adam by the name of sanctifying grace:

> When the Council of Trent teaches that the first Adam lost the holiness and righteousness in which he had been established ... this means that before sin, man possessed sanctifying grace with all the supernatural gifts that make man "righteous" before God. We may sum all this up by saying that, at the beginning, man was in friendship with God (Catechesis, 3 September 1986).

"CONSTITUTED" OR "CREATED" IN HOLINESS AND JUSTICE?

Another sidelight on the wording of the draft is the skirmish about the time when Adam received the initial grace. Was it with birth, or was it some time later? The draft had once stated that Adam was "created" in the supernatural state. That would mean he was never in a merely natural state, but was endowed with grace from the time when God created him. By substituting the term "constituted," in place of "created" the final version allowed freedom for an opinion held by partisans (but not by Thomas) that God created Adam in a natural state and allowed him to experience that for a time, before He elevated him to the supernatural state (cf. ST I,95,1). Peter Lombard and the Franciscan school taught that our first parents had to prepare themselves to receive sanctifying grace. God provided them initially with only the so-called preternatural gifts, so they held. God also assisted them with actual grace to prepare themselves for the reception of the crowning gift of sanctifying grace. Trent adroitly side-stepped the controversy by use of the word constituted. It doesn't state whether God created Adam in grace or bestowed it on him later (cf. Matthias Scheeben, p. 226).

Heinricus Renckens, SJ, (pp. 156 ff.) argues that the author of Genesis intended to teach us that God created Adam initially in the natural state only. He then raised him to the supernatural state when He brought Adam into the Garden of Eden. Genesis signifies this by relating that God first made Adam outside of the Garden, and led him into it only later. The Garden of Eden is seen as God's family garden, much as Persian kings owned private gardens for the exclusive use of their families. Walls prevented access by outsiders. When God took Adam into His garden, this indicated that God adopted him into His family by bestowing sanctifying grace on him. God conversed familiarly and intimately with Adam thereafter, as with a family member.

At any rate, the Fathers of Trent changed the draft to read "constituted" in place of "created." We see that they took their theological debates seriously.

"PRETERNATURAL GIFTS"

Trent dropped from its sober definitions any reference whatsoever to an alleged paradise filled with wonders. The Fathers excluded, for example, this high-flown description of paradise which had been circulated among them in a preliminary draft:

> "God made man right and incorruptible" (Eccles. 7:29, Sap. 2:23). This He did in regard to body, soul, mind, and spirit. In regard to the body He made him sound and integrated, not subject to corruption and death, nor exposed to labors, sorrows, and infirmities; in regard to the soul He made him well composed, integrated and tempered by righteousness and justice; the body was completely subject to the soul, the soul's lower powers where the passions are born were subject to its higher powers where reason reigns, as the proper order of well constituted nature required; in a marvelous manner the lower powers consented to the higher powers without any resistance, and the higher powers, that is reason and the mind itself, obediently submitted to God the creator, as was right.
>
> For that reason, though they were naked "they were not ashamed" (Gen 2:25), there being no reason for shame, since nothing in them opposed decency and reason" (*Con. Trid. edidit Societas Goerresiana* Vol.

XII, pp. 566-569; translation by author. See also Andre-Marie Dubarle, OP, p. 232).

The fact that a draft describing alleged gifts of integrity in
Adam was circulated among the Fathers of Trent suggests
that some among them had hoped the Council would
describe such a paradise in its definition. This the Council
did not do. Did they lack confidence that the paradise as
described above is revealed doctrine? The Fathers did not
deny that such a paradise existed, but neither did they
teach positively that it did exist.

Theories about an original paradise had indeed stirred the
imaginations of theologians and orators to sing ever new
glories about its salubrious climate with ever blooming
flowers, of forests filled with song birds. Trent's definitions have none of this. In the final definition the supposed
angelic state of Adam in an original paradise is totally omitted, and there is no description whatsoever of Adam's
condition before the Fall.

Trent also softened greatly the phrases of the preparatory
draft which alleged that the sin resulted in catastrophic
wounds of body and soul for Adam. Canon 1 now reads
only that "the whole Adam, body and soul, was changed
for the worse through the offence of his sin." That sentence was lifted literally from Orange II (see DS 371; Dupuis 504). Trent uses the words but does not spell out the
meaning in detail. Was there a change other than a loss of
grace and the breakdown of spiritual solidarity in the human race? The sentence provides fertile ground for theological speculation. The *CCC* does not mention a "tree of
life" with miraculous powers in paradise, nor does it use
the term "preternatural gifts." The wording of the text (No.

374-376) ascribes special efficacy to the original "radiance of grace" which brought inner harmony to man, to the union of man and woman, and with all of creation, without explicitly teaching that the condition was miraculous, over and above the effects of the "radiance of grace."

THE FINAL DEFINITION OF "CONCUPISCENCE"

The result of the debate on concupiscence was neatly defined in Canon 5 which reads in part:

> If anyone denies that the guilt of original sin is remitted by the grace of our Lord Jesus Christ given in Baptism, or asserts that all that is sin in the true and proper sense is not taken away but only brushed over or not imputed, anathema sit. For in those who are reborn God hates nothing...
>
> The holy Council, however, professes and thinks that concupiscence or the inclination to sin remains in the baptized. Since it is left for us to wrestle with, it cannot harm those who do not consent but manfully resist it by the grace of Jesus Christ. Rather, "one who strives lawfully will be crowned."...
>
> The Catholic Church has never understood that it is called sin because it would be sin in the true and proper sense in those who have been reborn, but because it comes from sin and inclines to sin. If anyone thinks the contrary, anathema sit (DS 1515; Dupuis 512).

Clearly, then, the Council defined what "concupiscence" is

not: it is not sin itself, nor is it sinful and hateful to God. Less clear is the definition about what it really is. Trent calls it an "inclination" to sin, which comes from sin and leads to sin. Two things here are noteworthy:

1) Trent does not state that concupiscence started suddenly with original sin as St. Augustine had claimed.

2) Nor does Trent state in so many words that concupiscence is anything other than our spontaneous and vigorous natural drives.

During the Tridentine debate this conundrum was proposed: "How can that (concupiscence) be bad which belongs to human nature?" No one came forward to answer that. Trent's final definition states more clearly what concupiscence is not than what it is.

Chapter 9

NAKED WITHOUT SHAME

Trent rejected the crass pessimism which claimed helplessness of the free will against irresistible onslaughts of concupiscence. Our free wills were not destroyed by the sin, Trent defined, and we remain responsible for our moral actions. Furthermore the Council omitted from its definitions exoteric versions of Adam's paradise as a kind of dreamland. Fortunately so. Such imaginary paintings of a heavenly paradise before the Fall followed by our alleged prosaic conditions after it, though pious in appearance, do not really help us in the struggle for spiritual goodness. Nostalgic imaginings of a "paradise lost" do not stir us to admire our present wonderful universe, and to sing its praises to God in thanksgiving. It can also seduce us into blaming Adam for our condition and so yielding to an attitude of fatalism which dulls determination for self-improvement and for striving to better the social life of mankind on earth.

The Fathers of Trent addressed no message of sympathy to mankind because of concupiscence. Instead they urged all to resist evil inclinations resolutely "by the grace of Jesus Christ" for "one who strives lawfully will be crowned" (canon 5). The formula of Trent, however, does not go all the way to state unambiguously that original sin did not damage our natural human endowments. St. Augustine had planted a dark view about the effect of original sin on human nature into theology, and to this day it is not completely dislodged. Folklore theology still inclines to describe concupiscence as a disorderly and evil tendency, an unfortunate distortion which troubles our natural drives and renders them unruly. The view that our sexual instinct is filthy, for example, is embedded vaguely into our perceptions. We say that we suffer this indignity because of Adam's sin.

Outstanding theologians today do not accept this archaic view. Our natures -- intellect, will, body, all our natural endowments -- are not disturbed due to original sin, they reason. Though original sin deprived us of bonus supernatural gifts, our natures survived the stripping of the gifts without suffering internal injury. The difference of our human nature before the sin and after is described as no more than the difference between a <u>nudus</u> and a <u>spoliatus</u> -- a nude body and a stripped body (see e.g. Canon J.M. Herve *Manuale Theologiae Dogmaticae* II, (1943), No. 447). The body remains the same in either case. We have every reason to agree with these theologians that our natures did not change when original sin stripped us of the very precious endowment of supernatural gifts, that ennoblement of the soul which capacitates us to strive for the reward of life with God in heaven after our testing on earth has been completed. St. Augustine's contrary theory reigned supreme in the field of theology for many centuries, but the time has come to purge this mistake from our midst.

St. Augustine latched on to the theory of damaged faculties in the heat of battle against the Pelagians who held overly optimistic views about the ability of humans to practice virtue without the help of grace. The saint may also have been influenced by his early tryst with the dualist Manichaeans, who believed in evil as an absolute force pervading creation. Finally, the converted sinner had experienced sexual intercourse only in an illegitimate union with a concubine, never in the state of holy Matrimony, and this may have contributed to his jaundiced view of the sexual drive. If he were alive today he might very well wish to write a "retractation," as he wrote retractions in his later years to modify some of his earlier works. We approach our task with humility, mindful that Augustine is an intellectual giant among men, and that he articulates truth with amazing insight.

EXPLANATION OF ST. AUGUSTINE

What the great St. Augustine once wrote in Chapter 13 of Book 13 of the *City of God* needs to be read with caution today:

> For, as soon as our first parents had transgressed the commandment, divine grace forsook them, and they were confounded at their own wickedness, and therefore they took fig leaves (which were possibly the first that came to hand in their troubled state of mind) and covered their shame; for though their members remained the same, they had shame now where they had none before. They experienced a new motion of their flesh, which had become disobedient to them, in strict retribution of their own disobedience to God. For the soul, reveling in its own liberty, and scorning to serve God, was itself deprived of the command it had formerly maintained over the body. And because it had willfully deserted its superior Lord, it no longer held its own inferior servant; neither could it hold the flesh subject, as it would always have been able to do had it remained itself subject to God. Then began the flesh to lust against the Spirit (Gal 5,-

17), in which strife we are born, deriving from the
first transgression a seed of death, and bearing in
our members, and in our vitiated nature, the con-
test or even victory of the flesh.

The passage indicates that Augustine attributed to Adam
and Eve the kind of motor control over their sexual and
other drives which we exercise over our movements of
hand and foot. They could start them and stop them at
will. The saint speculates in this manner consistently in
related chapters in *The City of God*. If that was Adam's
condition before the sin, then he became quite a different
type of human being after the sin; and we are all constituted quite differently than would have been our lot if Adam
had not sinned. But is it true?

The passage about nakedness without shame in Genesis
was the pivotal Scriptural text on which Augustine based
his explanation. The Church today acknowledges the use
of symbolism in Genesis (cf. Humani Generis, 1950; *Catechism of the Catholic Church*, No.375, 390, 396). St.
Augustine's great mind labored much under the constraints
of a literal interpretation. He admitted what is called a uni-
pluralism of the literal sense (cf. Bertrand de Margerie,
S.J., p.71), but did not allow himself to depart from inter-
preting Genesis as a historical chronology in a literal sense.
He wrote: "We believe the strict truth of the history, confirmed by its circumstantial narrative of facts" (*City of
God,* 13,21). The great Augustine wrote this before the
Church recognized that Genesis 1-11 is a special form of
history. The sacred author of Genesis very likely attached
just the opposite meaning to his words "naked without
shame" than Augustine read into them; he did not read the
Hebrew language in which the passage was first written.

NAKEDNESS WITHOUT SHAME IS SIN

A quite unflattering interpretation of the nakedness of Adam and Eve is as follows: although they are obviously dependent upon God (naked), they refuse to acknowledge this dependency (they lack shame). Like the serpent, they are devious.

Nakedness elsewhere in the Bible typically indicates utter dependence, helplessness, weakness, lack of self-help, derision by on-lookers, disgrace, inability to defend oneself, need of rescue and assistance, punishment for sin. Never elsewhere in the Bible does nakedness appear in a good light. Outside of this Genesis context, the word naked appears 43 times in the Old and New Testament. The companion word nakedness appears 54 times (cf. John Strong *Exhaustive Concordance of the Bible*, p.704). Nowhere in all these passages does nakedness ever designate virtue or self control. Naked and nakedness always describe quite the opposite, namely sin, punishment for sin, defeat, slavery, prostitution, betrayal of the covenant, sometimes a situation displeasing to God and arousing His wrath.

Job was born naked from his mother's womb (1:21), dependent upon her for everything, for food, warmth, affection. The Israelites danced naked around the golden calf (Ex 32:25) in a sex orgy, rebelling against the God who was giving the Ten Commandments to Moses at that very time on top of Mount Horeb. Isaiah walked around stark naked before the Israelites to dramatize that captives would be taken away "naked and barefoot with buttocks uncovered" (Is 20:4).

Ezekiel dramatized how the Lord will punish Israel for

whoring with false gods, for her unfaithfulness to the covenant, by exposing her genitals: "I will gather them against you from all sides and expose you naked for them to see" (Ez 16:37).

Christ promised a reward to those who found Him "naked" and gave Him clothes (Mt 25:36). Nowhere in the Old and New Testament is nakedness ever associated with virtue. The interpretation given by St. Augustine that nakedness without shame in Genesis 2:25 is a sign of virtue has no support from the rest of the Bible. "The Old Testament supplies no trace of the existence, among the sacred writers of any interpretation of the Fall-story comparable to the later doctrine of the Fall" [given by St. Augustine and others] writes F.R. Tennant (*The Sources of the doctrines of the Fall and Original Sin*, p.93).

If Genesis 2:25 presents our Adam and Eve as sinners-about-to-be, then their nakedness without shame fits the context smoothly. Being "naked without shame" would indicate sheer insensitivity to their absolute dependence upon God, whether from lack of experience, or from incipient pride.

Exegete John S. Kselman therefore asserts that the Hebrew text uses nakedness without shame as a symbol of the beginning of the sin of Adam and Eve. The pun in the text associates their "naked" condition (arummim) with the "cunning" (arum) of the serpent. Verse 25 of Chapter 2 ought to be verse 1 of Chapter 3, he writes, because it begins the story of the sin.

Adam and Eve should have shown their awareness of this "dependence on God who provides in the garden for their needs" (Kselman, "Genesis" in *Harper's Bible Commentary*, p.88). When the sacred author indicates that the man and woman were naked but not ashamed, he indicates thereby that they were at fault; not unlike some "gays" today, Adam and Eve "outed" their nakedness in defiance of God.

By not acknowledging their creaturehood and dependency, they were now poised to take the next step, which was explicit disobedience to God's commandment. Their pride was a prelude to the Fall. It is as Jeremiah will accuse Israel: "You have the brazen look of a prostitute. You refuse to blush with shame" (3:3; *NIV*).

The man and woman aspire to "be like God," to assert a godliness which was not theirs. It is a challenge to spread out wings and fly. In vain! What they learn instead, is that they are naked: "weak, vulnerable, and helpless, having rejected their dependence upon God" (Kselman, ibid.). The sin-experience forced their eyes open. They now saw what they had been pretending not to see: "Then the eyes of them both were opened, and they knew that they were naked; and they sewed fig leaves together and made themselves aprons." But their nakedness was not of a kind which clothing could hide. Adam, though covered, still felt naked before God: "I heard the sound of thee in the garden, and I was afraid, because I was naked." This was a nakedness of spirit, not of body.

That "naked without shame" points to a pretensive sham rather than to virtue fits in neatly with a separate insight of Saint Augustine that pride had preceded the Fall: "How could these words (of the serpent) persuade the woman that it was a good and useful thing that had been forbidden by God if there was not already in her heart a love of

her own independence and a proud presumption on self
...?" (*The Literal Meaning of Genesis,* II,11:30, trans. John
H. Taylor, The Newman Press, N.Y., 1982).

Their pride was a prelude to the Fall. That interpretation
harmonizes with the rest of the Bible which never associates nakedness with virtue. If nakedness without shame is
a symbol of insubordination, then Augustine's interpretation misses the point the author of Genesis makes here.
His theory about motor control over the passions and
emotions then vanishes into thin air, deprived of a biblical
foundation.

The Fathers of Trent respected Augustine greatly -- as is
only proper -- but did not incorporate this part of his theology into their definitions. They knew well enough what he
had written. Earlier drafts of their propositions about the
effects of original sin had reflected Augustinian leanings.
Adam was allegedly nearly an angel. Spontaneous movements of the passions were far from his august nature.
The Fathers of Trent expunged such preliminary wordings
from their final definitions. They backed away from them.

St. Irenaeus, who read this same passage of Genesis,
came to an entirely different conclusion than St. Augustine
did. He saw in the passage an indication that Adam and
Eve were children, too young to feel the stirring of the sex
drive. They lacked age, maturity, and experience (*Proof of
the Apostolic Teaching* 12; *Ad. Haer.* III,22,4; IV,38,1-4).
If an explicit Apostolic Tradition had existed teaching that
Adam and Eve were adults without a spontaneous sex
drive, Irenaeus would not have missed it. This indicates
that the Augustinian position is not drawn from an explicit
Apostolic Tradition.

ROMANS: "SIN LIVES IN ME"

Paul's aphorism that sin lives within us as a kind of second life must be explained in a manner compatible with the rest of St. Paul's writings, and not contradictory to them. The explanation of the passage must also square with the rest of the Bible, which presents God as all holy, not one who seduces man into sin. It cannot be true that God Himself stirs up in us a seduction to commit sin. Yet the passage of Paul amazes us:

> I do not understand my own actions. For I do not do what I want, but I do the very thing I hate. Now if I do what I do not want, I agree that the law is good. So then it is no longer I that do it, but sin which dwells within me (Rom 15-17).

This sounds very much like St. Augustine's explanation that the passions within us are in a state of declared war against our reason, all because of original sin. Theologian Fr. Walter J. Burghardt, SJ once expressed the claim in the following dramatic manner:

> There was a striking unity, a fascinating harmony, within man himself: within Adam, within Eve. That grim, unceasing struggle which we experience within ourselves, which Paul described - flesh warring against spirit, lust against love, passion against purpose, all the schizophrenia that cleaves me into two - such conflict was foreign to Eden. Adam, like Eve, could not be seduced by surprise, could not say, as Paul would, "The very thing I hate, that is what I do" (Rom 7:15). An inner poise, a sanity and serenity, a profound oneness,

such was God's design; such was man to be (*The Catholic Mirror,* 26 September 1974).

Fr. William Most once illustrated the classic view in a similar manner as follows:

> However, there could be a superadded gift that would make all these drives, including sex, subject to reason. With it, each drive would wait for the orders of reason, and only then would it move. Now, since Adam before the fall had felt no problem from sex, no need of clothing, it is evident that he had such a special superadded gift. The theological name for it is: gift of integrity. It is equally obvious after the fall, when his nudity troubled him, that Adam had lost that gift (*National Catholic Register,* 13 July 1975).

I am inclined to believe that we make life harder for ourselves to no good purpose if we so describe life before the Fall as blissful and entirely free of trouble, whereas we blame our present hardships on the Fall. Do we not feed on self-pity to no purpose by so blaming original sin and Adam for present difficulties? Trent, as we saw, steered away from describing a painless paradise before the Fall. We do well to follow that example. Likewise Paul describes life after the Fall as victorious when lived with the help of Christ, not as a perpetual schizophrenia.

Paul, in the above passage, wrote about indecision <u>before</u> conversion, while the mind is still vacillating between a previous life of sin and a new call to conversion. "To regard this experience as remaining after conversion is against the whole line of the argument ... and against all the moral exhortations in Paul's epistles" (A. Thiesen and P. Byrne, "Romans" in *A New Commentary on Holy Scripture*, p. 1122). After conversion, Paul recognizes no "cleavage" between one's passions and a relationship with Christ: "For I am certain that nothing can separate us from his love..." (Rom 8:38).

Pain and pleasure experienced in our sensitive bodies should not be interpreted as a "cleavage" in our personalities. Surely Christ had no such "cleavage" in Himself when His feelings convulsed against the prospects of the passion and death which obedience to the Father required: "Father, if thou are willing, remove this from me; nevertheless, not my will, but thine, be done" (Lk 22:42). Christ never swerved from obedience. His revulsion against the pain was not some split personality within Him, and did not break His resolve to remain obedient. From this we can conclude that, when we feel reluctance to pay the cost of obedience, this is not necessarily an effect of original sin. When we believe that the state of grace enables us to remain masters of our moral life, we do not imply that grace automatically takes over the automatisms of natural tendencies. Natural tendencies are completely normal when they shrink from pain and when they reach out for pleasure. It is normal for them to function as they are constituted, even when their tendencies are not in harmony with the dictates of the moral life to which we are called by supernatural grace.

Pope John Paul II noted that a spiritual struggle does not necessarily destroy peace of mind. Quoting the above passage of Rom 7:19,22,23, he observes that "original sin and our personal sins" have occasioned a vigorous struggle within us. To this he adds: "But this conflict does not exclude the person's deep peace of mind: 'Thanks be to God through Jesus Christ our Lord!...I myself serve the law of God with my mind'(Rom 2:25)" (To the Cardinal Major Penitentiary, 20 May, 1998).

We look in vain in Romans and in Paul's other writings for a teaching that concupiscence is an evil tendency implanted into us by God. What Paul says is that these instincts remain natural only, and so will lead us away from God if the will enslaves itself to them. It is our task, writes Paul, to make the spirit master over the proclivities of nature: "Do not present the parts of your bodies to sin as weapons for wickedness, but present yourselves to God as raised from the dead to life and the parts of your bodies to God as weapons for righteousness" (Rom 6:13).

A NON-MIRACULOUS EXPLANATION IS PREFERABLE

A non-miraculous explanation of the primal innocence of Adam and Eve is possible. Theology has a rule of thumb that "miracles are not to be multiplied." We know that God endowed Adam and Eve initially with sanctifying grace. Together with grace He gave them the attached package of infused theological, intellectual, and moral virtues. He may even have imprinted on their brains the neurological pathways of pre-formed habits beneficial to the initial founders of human culture. With the help of grace, the imprinted habits could become stable virtues. But we have no reasonable evidence, and no convincing arguments, to demonstrate that our Adam and Eve had motor control over their emotional life and their normal human drives. Such equipment would have made our Adam a miracle man. Better said, a theological construct.

The meaning which Pope John Paul II gives to the status of Adam and Eve before the Fall can also be interpreted in this manner. Their love was not disturbed by their sex drive, he teaches. On the contrary, the "nuptial gift of the body" enhanced their spiritual love by resonating also in the body. This is normative for married couples today as well, he teaches (see especially the weekly catechesis delivered during September 5, 1979 - April 2, 1980.) The Pope thus proposes that what was normative for Adam and Eve in this respect, is normative in married life today. It was so in paradise, it is so today.

The Pope employs use of a special gift of "integrity" to explain his points. The *CCC* also alludes to it (No. 400). It is plausible to describe this gift as a positive influence of grace which enabled Adam and Eve to deal calmly and adequately with their drives, passions, and emotions. An annealment or closer bonding of reason to the passions, we may call it, by which reason could inhibit with ease the impulsive nature of the lively emotions. God may also have imprinted in Adam's brain the neurological pathways of good habits, which saints acquire with much labor during the course of life. Good habits are, from the physiological aspect, a modification of cerebral pathways. When informed with grace, they become virtues. Thus Adam, according to this view, was serenely and stably equipped to inhibit wayward movements of nature. The notion of imprinted habits informed with grace is sufficient to account for the so-called gift of "integrity" which is commonly attributed to Adam and Eve as founders of human culture. The concept of cerebrally imprinted habits in our first parents might appeal less to Irenaeus than to Augustine. Irenaeus preferred a youthful and inexperienced Adam whom God expected to strive for perfection, to learn through experience, and so to achieve maturity by personal effort. He had little respect for human character if it was not forged in the furnace of personal endeavor, but was handed over on a platter as a gift.

CONCUPISCENCE vs NATURAL HUMAN DRIVES

Eyes are obviously made for seeing whatever is to be seen, no matter if it be good or evil. If what they see excites the viewer to devious sexual appetites, or to greed and theft, the eyes care not at all. The eyes simply focus the incoming rays of light upon the retina's rods and cones, which in turn transmit the data into the brain for processing into vision. When this is done well, the eyes are doing their task perfectly. For this they are admirably designed and engineered. We do not expect the eyes to scramble the sight of tempting bodies, to censor for us what we ought not see. The eyes were not renovated by grace to transform tempting sights into holy pictures. Were that to happen, we would not be masters over our eyes, but they would master us.

Likewise the ears, the nose, the taste, and the touch organs are programmed to do their thing, and do it well. If they do not function as programmed, we suspect illness and consult a physician. When our drives operate in accordance with inbuilt structures and automatisms, as designed by God, we judge them to be healthy and normal.

To put it in another way: our drives are native and spontaneous atheists. Unless reason and will exercise control over them, they roam as they please. On their own, divorced from reason, they know absolutely nothing about God, about heaven, about the Ten Commandments. The sex drive is as ready to operate in a brothel as in a holy conjugal situation. All our senses, our instincts, our drives, if cut off from direction by our personhood, act like atheists. Only our minds and hearts can make them function as believers. Christ admonished us to master our interior household: "If your right eye causes you to sin, tear it out and throw it away. It is better for you to lose one of your members than to have your whole body thrown into Gehenna" (Mt 5:29). Again: "Enter through the narrow gate; for the gate is wide and the road broad that leads to destruction, and those who enter through it are many" (Mt 7:13-14). We are obligated to seek the high moral ground with our reason, and to curb our senses when they tend to gravitate to matters unreasonable.

LIVING IN THE AMBIGUITY OF INDECISION

The vacillation which Paul describes is a situation in which the subject lacks determination: "Now if I do what I do not want, it is no longer I who do it, but sin that dwells in me" (Rom 7:20). The drives appear to sense when the veto of the will is infirm. Their instinct is to persevere in order to gain their objective. Whereas when the drives are confronted by a wall of firm decision, fortified by grace, this renders their further action impotent, devoid of malice. A firm "NO!" may not stonewall the futile fire of passions, but it frees us from responsibility about their continued presence. If they operate against the consent of the will, there is no sin, no guilt.

St. Augustine, in his classic *Confessions* illustrates the "schizophrenic" mind-set typical of one who hesitates between good and evil. He feared that by requesting God's grace he might lose the sweet taste of sin:

Being enamored of a happy life, I yet feared it in its own abode, and, fleeing from it, sought after it. I conceived that I should be too unhappy were I deprived of the embracements of a woman; and of Thy merciful medicine to cure that infirmity I thought not, not having tried it. As regards continency, I imagined it to be under the control of my own strength (though I myself found it not), being so foolish as not to know what is written, that none can be continent unless Thou give it (Wis 8:2); and that Thou wouldst give it, if with heartfelt groaning I should knock at Thine ears, and should with firm faith cast my care upon Thee (6:11).

He did begin to pray for chastity later, but "schizophrenically." He prayed for chastity but "not yet." As of now, he chose pleasure. He tells how he found it "impossible" to be chaste only because he indulged in pleasures of unchastity willingly. He hesitated to shake himself free from "the unruly habit saying to me: 'Dost thou think thou canst live without them?'" (*Confessions* 8,11).

A much relieved Augustine could pray after his conversion: "Now was my soul free from the gnawing cares of seeking and getting, and of wallowing and exciting the itch of lust" (*Confessions* 9,1). He was no longer schizophrenic, but felt that he was in control. He learned by dramatic experience that he cannot do it alone, that he stands in need of grace. Torn in two while he left the drives to have their way, he had yearned indecisively for self control. This division ceased when he prayed and with God's grace took control of himself.

CONCLUSION

The phrase in Genesis 2:28 "they were both naked and were not ashamed," when interpreted symbolically rather than literally as here explained, collapses the theory of Augustine that Adam and Eve had motor control over the sex instinct and other natural drives before their sin. Our natural human drives -- another term for "concupiscence" -- can then be viewed as being intrinsically undisturbed by original sin. Humans today do not experience a notable change of body when they lose the state of grace by one mortal sin. It may not have been essentially different in Adam's case. The sin deprived Adam of the gift of grace, but this deprivation plausibly did not damage his nature directly. This allows us to accept our nature with gratitude from God, as healthy, as normal, and as admirably designed by the Creator to assist us in our daily living while on earth.

Chapter 10

BIOLOGY AND "CONCUPISCENCE"

MOTOR CONTROL OF THE PASSIONS?

We ask next why our human nature is so composed that the mind does not have direct control over the emotions. The structural design of the brain suggests that this is not a result of original sin. As we saw, St. Augustine theorized that Adam and Eve "experienced a new motion of their flesh which had become disobedient to them" because of their sin (*City of God* 13:13), but it is a theory which is difficult to defend today.

Rather than looking for a change in the physical biology of humans due to original sin, we should locate the reason for our moral weakness in the dynamics of human cooperation with the grace of God. We believe that when humans disobey God and commit mortal sin, as Adam and Eve did, they deprive themselves thereby of the state of sanctifying grace. It happens only too easily that they then become easy victims of various other temptations to sin. In this situation man stands in utter need of rescue by God.

When the sinner converts, when he receives God's forgiveness and His grace, he becomes equipped once more to persevere in this condition of restored supernatural life, though he may have to contend with determination against self-acquired vice. Although he is thus healed personally, the social condition of the human race in whose midst he lives is now marked by original sin. Racial solidarity of obedience to God remains shattered. The fashion of sin in society is difficult to resist, much as fashions in dress and other social behavior draw us powerfully toward social conformity. Rebellion against God, or simple discounting of His sovereignty, remain regrettably fashionable in much of human society. In this chapter we explore, with the aid of biological data, why it is normal that tension between our reason and our natural drives persist even when we are in the state of grace. What Trent termed "concupiscence" is seen to be normal and healthy natural drives functioning as they ought. Because they are natural and attuned to earthly life, they continue to operate after Baptism like before, subject only to the "political" governance of the will and modification by the influence of grace. Their natural function oftentimes brings them into conflict with our supernatural calling to transform our lives on earth into a training session for entrance into heaven.

St. Thomas Aquinas (1225-1274), the next intellectual Olympus in the Church after St. Augustine, generally agreed with his great predecessor that original sin must have done something to cut off control by the mind over the emotions. Like Augustine, he felt bound to interpret Genesis quite literally as did the other great thinkers of their time. The Church had not yet given guidance that Genesis 1-11 is not interpreted correctly as the kind of chronological history which has become traditional since Greek and Roman times. The interpreters who had misunderstood the sense of Genesis concluded with misled logic that if Adam and Eve could stand before each other naked and not feel sexual tension, they must have had very direct control of mind over matter. God subsequently deprived man of this privilege because of original sin, so they concluded. And in punishment for original sin man has now to use effort and good sense to keep the unruly emotions corralled in some semblance of domestic peace.

St. Thomas, following the lead of the brilliant Greek philosopher Aristotle (384-422 BC), described our limited domination of the passions by the term "political control:"

> Hence the Philosopher (Aristotle) says (Polit. 1,2) that the reason governs the irascible and concupiscible not by a despotic supremacy which is that of a master over his slave, but by a politic and royal supremacy, whereby the free are governed, who are not wholly subject to command" (ST I-II,17,7).

Political control is a good description of what our minds can now do in relation to the emotions. Our reason can agree or disagree with the spontaneous movements of instincts and emotions, can assent or dissent, can wish them to quiet down, can seek to distance their functioning from their source of stimulation, cut the line of perception, can busy the brain with attention to other business while the neglected passions then run out of energy. But as politics go, so also our control of the passions has its ups and downs, partial successes and partial failures. Through firm determination on part of the will and by means of sagacious political maneuvers, we do manage to get along fairly well with our passions. We depend upon our perceptions constantly to maintain our awareness, for they are our allies, essential to support our faculty to make free decisions.

But motor control over the passions eludes our efforts. Whether we like it or not, whether we agree or disagree, our pride, our greed, the sex drive, anger, appetite for food and drink, envy of the neighbor, our laziness and tendency to escape duties, our unruly ambitions for undeserved or destructive fame -- all this "concupiscence" is equipment by which we live out our personal lives and by which society functions. Like ever changing weather, they occasion frustration as well as joy.

These very same drives which capacitate us for normal life can with equal aplomb threaten our own self interests, our love of God and neighbor, as well as the common good of society. None of these drives obey commands to start or stop instantly as do the more pliant movements of hand and foot which are under motor control. When a king commands his daughter to marry and love a prince, she can do the marrying in a ceremony, but she may not be able to obey her father to generate emotions of love. Emotions are chronically allergic against control by dictator reason, like children who always learn to say NO before they learn the word YES. The emotions operate on automatisms which are not under immediate motor control of the will.

Even if we did have motor control over our passions -- even if we could, for example, stop envying the neighbor by command of the will -- would we always be willing to do that? The angels who were not encumbered by passions of a body were able to decide for good or evil, yet not all of them chose what is good. Which suggests that even if our reason and will would have motor control over sentiments of pride and ambition, that alone might not guarantee that we choose correctly. Genesis teaches that our still flawless Adam and Eve fell during their very first trial. In the final analysis, our decisions are made not by passions, but by our reasoning selves who are free, who have these passions as part of our life equipment.

THE EMOTIONS AND THE TRIUNE BRAIN

We invoke the help of specialists to provide information about brain structures and the neural substratum which houses the emotions. Our brain is remotely comparable to a thousand telephone switchboards, each serving a gigantic megapolis, whirling with the activity of generating, receiving and transmitting messages. "Through its incredible ability to hook together thousands of reverberating circuits in a fraction of a second -- each representing a memory of an idea -- the brain is able to bring together into one grand circuit the data needed to think and make decisions" (Bruce Bliven, 52).

The three main sections of the brain are said to reflect a three stage evolution:

1) The basic ganglia or stembrain. It is sometimes called the "reptilian" section. This regulates the basic body functions.

2) The midbrain or limbic system. Called also the "mammalian" section, it is the seat of the emotions.

3) The neocortex or forebrain. It is said to be the newest part, the specifically human section. We use it to think and to exercise free choice. It is not set into the cogwheels of the emotions whirling in the midbrain, but acts as a benign though sometimes aloof boss of the limbic complex.

The stembrain controls basic life functions such as breathing, heart beat, endocrine output, general metabolism. It can continue to operate even when the forebrain computer is down.

The midbrain is the biological agency of our emotions (read concupiscence). Its circuits support our activities of love, joy, tenderness, hatred, sadness, envy, pride, ambition. The midbrain is said to have developed during early mammalian life. Mammals have more emotional capacity than do reptiles.

The neocortex or forebrain is distinctly human, a species specific later addition to the older mammalian and reptile brains. It capacitates humans for rational and linguistic operations. Geographic areas of this neocortex are mapped for their specific functions, such as abstraction and speech, for motor control of foot, body, hand, face, eye, and areas which process vision, hearing and other functions. Yet none of these neocortex areas operate as isolated performers. Whenever they operate they do so in vital connection with the entire brain.

As Philip Lieberman notes: "Although some brain mechanisms may be language specific, we cannot assume that all brain mechanisms involved in human language constitute an isolated organ." And although human language and thought probably are the "newest" attributes of Homo Sapiens, their brain bases are not restricted to only the phylogenetically newest parts of the brain. Though we undoubtedly have specialized neural organs, mechanisms that evolved to facilitate cognitive and linguistic activities, these in turn developed from simpler and earlier organs which had supported less complicated functions. And the more newly developed areas "usually continue to participate in the older, simpler patterns of behavior as well as in the newer, derived cognitive activity" (*Uniquely Human,* 1991, p. 15).

The thinking brain, mainly our neocortex, operates in biological conjunction with the emotive midbrain, as well as with the basic life ganglia of the stembrain. It cannot operate by itself, without the combined assistance of the midbrain as a working partner, and of the stembrain as the supplier of life energy. The entire brain family must be present and willing if the forebrain is to do any thinking and willing.

But the midbrain is different. It can operate without the neo-cortex. We can emote without thinking. However, the midbrain cannot operate without input from the stembrain. We cannot emote with the midbrain unless the basic ganglia keep us alive by operating the vital functions.

The stembrain can keep us alive by itself, even when the two higher brain compartments are asleep or out of action. We have, therefore, three brain compartments, the rational forebrain, the emotive midbrain, and the vital stembrain.

THE SEX DRIVE, GATEWAY TO ALL EMOTIONS

Jerome Lejeune notes that the forebrain projection of the genital organs is at the upper extremity of the Rolando fissure in the interhemispheric surface, very close to the midbrain. It is therefore the one and only cortical representation to be in contact with the limbic locale of emotions; this is the crossroads of the drives needed for the preservation of life (hunger, thirst, aggression) and the drives needed for the preservation of the species (reproduction, protection of the young, love). It follows that we are so constituted that whatever concerns genital activity involves also moral activity, neurologically speaking. This points to the impossibility of mastering emotional behavior if we do not first master conscious and deliberate genital behavior (cf. Lejeune, "Is there a natural morality?" in *Linacre Quarterly,* 1989).

Professor Lejeune here makes the significant observation that voluntary sexual discipline is the gateway through which we must pass to take control of emotional life. The very important conclusion follows that one who governs his sexual appetite reasonably well is thereby in the key position to control all the emotions. He will likely also control fairly well greed, envy, anger, love, hatred, sadness. Boys achieve virtuous manhood, girls develop well-behaved womanhood first and foremost by disciplining themselves in proper sexual behavior on the way to adulthood.

The intense struggle to control the emerging sex drive which every boy and girl experiences during the process of growing to maturity is a moral necessity imposed by God and nature. Temptations are strong, keen, lasting, sometimes unexpected, utterly flattering to heart and mind. Years of struggle does not tame them. Yet by mastering them with firm and constant resolve - and by rising again and again after a fall - we acquire the bonus reward of tempering all our other natural drives in tandem with the sex drive. This indicates how very beneficial it is for adolescents to be educated in chastity and encouraged to practice it with unbending resolve. It also indicates how great is the evil of those who scandalize youth by imparting sex education in a manner which arouses passions and inculcates no values. Without disciplining the sex drive, youths fail to form strong moral characters, and society as whole deteriorates. The human community enjoys distinct advantages when its members act reliably and responsibly:

when airline pilots practice sobriety and study to remain competent, when bankers are honest, when laborers do their job well. By stirring up unruly sex habits in youth, faulty sex educators tend to collapse individual and social reliability in the entire population of the next generation. We are all losers if a generation of juveniles is influenced against disciplined sexual mores. Youths who do not keep a tight rein on their sex drive lose much control over other areas of character development.

Adolescents who surrender their neo-cortical freedom by yielding to sexual abandon, thereby stunt growth toward emotional maturity. The body may grow into adulthood, while emotional childishness persists. The sex playboy may also be a thief because of greed, a drug addict because of low self-image, a cheater in games, a copycat in examinations, a liar who will not admit that it was he who "cut down the cherry tree." Even though the body grows big into adulthood, the character remains a cretin, a playboy in a grown body.

Lejeune draws this implication about behavior from the fact that neurologically the projection of the genital organs in the extremity of the Rolando fissure of the neocortex is situated as a gateway into the limbic system which is the theater of concupiscence, of the emotions. In other words, he who controls this gateway of genital activity gains the upper hand in dominating all the restive emotional drives and powers. He controls the strategic gateway between rational life and animal life.

MOTOR CONTROL OF EMOTIONS?

Augustine spoke of an alleged ability by innocent Adam to

call the emotions into action when reason and free will want them to go into operation. He postulated likewise that reason can stop their action on command. That concept translated into brain functions would indicate that the forebrain overrides the midbrain when it issues a command. But that is not the way our brain functions today.

Today the emotive midbrain operates antecedently to the forebrain. It capacitates the forebrain for action. The forebrain does not simply control midbrain and stembrain at will. Quite the opposite, unless the midbrain takes an initiative, the forebrain is paralyzed. Only after the midbrain capacitates the forebrain for action can this forebrain begin to influence the midbrain. Once capacitated, the forebrain can inhibit activities of the midbrain. It can tone down some activities directly to a certain extent. It can also divert attention away from its exciting object to thus shut down the midbrain's heated activities indirectly. The higher cortex, the seat of reason and will, is more effective in inhibiting the free flow of the emotional functions than in initiating them, explains Msgr. Timothy Gannon, following Paul Maclean:

> The cortical centers are much more effective in inhibiting the free flow of these functions than in initiating them... It is as if the commands of reason are too harsh and too abstract to be translated directly into behavior (Gannon 28; 30).

The degree of autonomy exercised by the brainstem over the ongoing functions of life, such as heart beat and regulation of the blood sugar, makes direct control of its functions by the cortex impossible. The stembrain does all this without need of conscious direction by the forebrain. This allows the forebrain freedom to pursue intellectual activities without need of overseeing breathing and heartbeat and basic vital activities.

Between the life functions controlled by the stem, and the thinking functions seated in the cortex, is the midbrain area which processes emotions. It is to this area that our attention is drawn in our discourse about concupiscence. If today our neocortex cannot exercise complete motor control over the neurological activity of the limbic midbrain, nor of the brainstem, then how did Adam do so unless his brain was structured differently than ours is? That is, unless his forebrain could override the midbrain and stembrain.

If Adam had our kind of brain, but could draw directly on spiritual powers to activate or deactivate the limbic midbrain and the brainstem, he would be a "miracle man." He could at will simply by-pass normal biological processes by means of powers of the spirit. We might call it "mind-over-matter" or angelic powers.

The other alternative is that he would use not spiritual powers but biological operations to govern his emotions with instant motor control. His neocortex would then use neurological pathways to overrule the limbic system. If Adam could do that, then his brain structure would have been essentially different from our own. That would necessitate an entire restructuring of all other bodily functions. Even so, it wouldn't function. Such an Adam would be a piece of biological junk.

Gannon explains how the limbic midbrain mediates to make the neocortex aware. In subsequent response, it adapts the commands of the neocortex to the biological capacities of the body's organs. We might imagine that Adam's neocortex could take command of the midbrain to override its mediatory functions, in order to evoke obedient action from it. But that would require more than natural powers. Gannon writes:

> And this is precisely how we experience emotions; as an awareness intervening between the clear dictates of reason and the appetites controlled by lower centers... To speak of sexual functions as if they could be turned on or off by a simple directive of reason ... is a grave error...The whole triune brain functions as a unit with the three levels completely integrated (Gannon, 30;31.).

The Augustinian concept would have the reason (neocortex) take the initiative of calling emotions into action, or shutting off their activities. But our brain functions exactly in the opposite sequence. It is the feelings housed in the midbrain which serve up to the reason housed in the neocortex an awareness of what is going on. This arranges the stage upon which the mind can then make choices. The intermediary limbic lobe is, in turn, closely connected with the stembrain below it, constantly initiating or mediating orders to the stem, and in turn receiving stimuli from it. As Gannon explains:

> As the feelings and emotions arise in consciousness they bring with them an awareness of the self, the awareness of how we feel about the activity in question, and an incipient movement toward or away from it. This pattern of the manner in which the brain functions also goes a long way

in helping us to accept the paradox ... that it is the feelings and emotions that make the brain work, rather than the other way around (Gannon, 30.).

Emotions cannot function in the brain alone but are in vital dependence upon the physical teamwork of the entire body. Thus the emotion of anger, agitating the nerves in the midbrain, stimulates the stem brain to send a message to the adrenal glands to produce and pour into the blood stream a series of hormonal stimuli which are targeted for the receptors in different organs of the body. Anger is not a mere "tempest in a teapot" of the brain, but involves myriads of supporting systems and operations in the body. To support the anger and to make it physically effective, the body then ups the tempo of the heart-beat, increases the concentration of sugar in the blood to fuel the muscle fibers, tenses the muscles, increases alertness of eyes and ears, flushes the face, perhaps erects hairs in their follicles and flashes lightning from the eyes.

To illustrate the magnitude of the operation -- comparable on a mini-scale with initiating and maintaining the logistics of the D-Day Invasion of the Normandy Coast -- we draw attention to only one of the many items involved, the sugar content in the blood. To do battle when angry, the blood sugar is consumed at a higher rate than when the body is at emotional rest. The level of sugar in the blood is critical to total bodily health. We pay a great price if the sugar level gets even slightly off balance: "Sugar is one of the body's energy producing substances and we must have just the right amount, no more and no less. We walk a biological tightrope between coma [insufficient sugar] and convulsion [excess of sugar], the possible results of relatively light changes in blood-sugar levels (John Edward

Pfeiffer, M.D., "Introducing the Brain" p. 47). The brain keeps us alive by monitoring the systems continuously and keeping them in balance.

If Adam had been capable of giving direct orders to his body to be angry, or to stop anger instantly, he would likely have made impossible demands upon his biological system. Our system functions best when the commands of the neocortex are filtered through and seconded by the limbic midbrain, which in turn excites the reactions in the stembrain which then makes the body cooperate in accordance with the orders of the remote "commander in chief." As a result, the passions may appear to be "stubborn" or irrationally persistent. But we should recognize that there is a biological reason for this "irrational persistence." Complex and time-consuming biological processes necessarily result in a "fly-wheel" governing modification of the passions. A response cannot be instant, but only gradual; the flywheel goes into motion slowly at its own pace. Neither will the flywheel stop instantly when once in full motion.

The body must provide the biological basis for any and every action which is tinged with emotion. It supports anger with a modification of the organism which equips it for a battle, or for defeat in helpless frustration. The entire body needs to be adjusted to perform a sexual episode, to generate a spasm of envy, to knot the body in hate, to expand the emotion of love. If Adam would suddenly stop the emotion during mid-performance, there would be no combustion of the abnormal amount of blood sugar, the heightened tension of the muscles would remain unrelaxed, the body would go into convulsions, perhaps into shock and a life-threatening situation. He would poison his systems with uncombusted deposits. Contrary to a popular misunderstanding that the passions are in disorder as a result of original sin, we ought to recognize the limitations of our physiological nature. Our biological system is marvelously constructed to serve our emotions, and the emotions are faithful supporters of thinking brain. Adam's sin has not, I believe, disturbed our physiological condition.

If we suppose that Adam had motor control over the emotions and drives and instincts -- over concupiscence -- either his brain and body functioned differently than ours, or he had spiritual powers by which he could override the biological circuits, akin to what we will have after the resurrection. Neither of these explanations satisfies us. If his brain and body functioned differently than ours does, then he was not of our species, and we are not his descendants. If he had spiritual powers like a resurrected body, then he belonged to the angel world, not to our world of mortals. An angel is not our ancestor.

CHILDREN MODEL THEIR LIVES ON PARENTS

Augustine confessed that he had found it exceedingly difficult to break out of his habit of sin. Once he had this habit it became a kind of second nature to him. Its demands were impetuous, taking over a kind of secondary control of his mind and body. His father had not educated him to control his sexual appetite. In fact, his father had noted with pride signs of his sexual prowess, whereas his mother ineffectively warned him against fornication and especially adultery. Had both father and mother educated him effectively by word and example to be chaste, and had his neighbors, his village, his school, his parish, his entire known environment expected him to be chaste, then perhaps he would have chosen to live chastely from the beginning. Solidarity in virtue practiced all around him may have motivated him to be always chaste. That is also the logic of a paradise without sin: if the entire community would practice virtue in complete solidarity, its exercise would become easier for each individual.

If all parents in the world would control concupiscence and educate their children by word and example to do likewise; and if all members of social structures and all administrators of government would converge in solidarity to make the ten commandments dominate in private and public life; and if the entire human family would then adore the Lord their God faithfully, it would be easier for all to say with Paul: "In all things we conquer overwhelmingly through him who loved us" (Rom 8:37). But original sin has shattered this solidarity of the human race in the universal practice of virtue.

When parents educate their children well, especially now when original sin affects social life, they make it easier for the children to practice virtue thereafter. Learning virtue when young is like learning a language during childhood. Whatever language there be, the child is equal to it. It can learn any of the thousands of languages in the world, be it English, Japanese, Chinese, Swahili, or any other listed on the plaque of the Tower of Babel. And it soon speaks in the local dialect.

In much the same way we see children acting like their parents, and take on the behavioral pattern of the extended family and of the surrounding community. Their brains are initially habit-neutral, so to speak, plastic and elastic enough to be molded into habits of good or habits of evil. Children refuse, however, to have virtue imprinted upon them. Outsiders can provide models and motivation, but each child must do its own imprinting.

BEHAVIOR MODIFIES NEURAL AUTOMATISMS

Dr. med. Josef Roetzer quotes the famous dictum that "the mind molds the brain" (see Roetzer, "Humanae Vitae," p. 769). Brain researcher Wilder Penfeld had coined the phrase which calls attention to the fact that the brain is subject to physical alteration by the teaching that parents give to their children, and by the personal efforts which the child and the adult make. For the molding of the brain to facilitate the practice of virtue is a lifetime task, though it is enormously easier to start well, than to make adjustments and corrections later in life.

Nobel prize winner John C. Eccles spoke of a self conscious mind which acts as a liaison brain to then mold the organ of the brain which we possess (cf. Roetzer, 769). We might say that this "liaison brain" is our conscious effort, is the work of a midwife, to facilitate the birth of habits. In other words, the ideal which we set before the brain can be the blue print which guides and stimulates the brain to shape itself accordingly.

To learn the ten commandments from our parents, then, is an advantage which expedites and simplifies the proper formation of the brain of the child. And the child who has initially learned correct conduct from the parents, has the task of on-going formation which it must continue on its own.

Man's appropriate organ for exercising choice is his unique brain. The brain can be regarded as the organ of man's personality. What he has experienced in his life, the considerations he has had to think over, the attitudes he has acquired - all these things accumulate in his brain. The brain must be molded and shaped in the right way if man is to use it as an organ of free will. We have already spoken of the moldable capacity, the plasticity, of the brain. We must consider the formational stages of the brain.

Take, for example, the mother-child relationship in the first years of a child's life. The child must experience mother's love in order to acquire the ability for social communication without fear or hate. You all know about the difficulties arising from disturbed people who perform acts of violence against society because - of course, that is in many cases only a part of the pertinent cause - they have not experienced the love of a mother in the formational period of the brain concerned with this attitude. The older a patient grows, the more difficult becomes therapy for any disturbed behavior, because the brain is successively losing its plasticity (Roetzer, 768-769).

The sin which Adam and Eve committed de-flowered the virginal seal of an inerrant development of virtue within themselves first of all. The molding of their brains to facilitate the practice of virtue was no longer guaranteed by lives of constant obedience to God's commandments. They, in turn, passed on their own deficiency to their offspring, not by the genetic route but by a distortion in the pattern of their education. In turn the community became adversely affected by ripple effects of disturbances, all of which became a part of the "sin of the world" into which we are born.

On the other hand, because we are free and God gives all the help we need, each of us can live virtuously and peacefully. Even the entire human family can rise and shine to create a global solidarity in virtue provided everybody cooperates. God, however, does not imprint such a solidarity upon our race. He offers us the joy of endeavoring to achieve it ourselves.

CONCLUSION

Parents should normally and routinely rebuild the wall around the Garden of Eden for their children. Within the Garden of the Home parents can shelter the children from the sinful world outside, and form them in virtue. Young children eagerly copy the behavioral model of their parents. Their good behavior in turn helps to mold the brain to facilitate virtue during adulthood.

The alleged mind-over-the-passions control of Adam and Eve which Augustine once taught is probably a biological impossibility. We have no proof that Adam and Eve controlled their emotional life in a manner other than we do. It is only after the resurrection that "the soul will...communicate to the body...impassibility and glory" (Thomas, *ST* I,97,3).

Until that time comes we can live in victorious tension with concupiscence, in a politically enforced peace, a peace which Christ gives us.

Chapter 11

HOW THE SIN IS TRANSMITTED

The *CCC* teaches that we inherit original sin from Adam, but adds that we do not understand the manner of transmisssion very well:

> **404.** How did the sin of Adam become the sin of all his descendants? The whole human race is in Adam "as one body of one man" (St. Thomas Aquinas, *De Malo* 4,1). By this "unity of the human race" all men are implicated in Adam's sin, as all are implicated in Christ's justice. Still, the transmission of original sin is a mystery that we cannot fully understand. But we do know by Revelation that Adam had received original holiness and justice not for himself alone, but for all human nature. By yielding to the tempter, Adam and Eve committed a *personal sin*, but this sin affected *the human nature* that they would transmit *in a fallen state* (Trent, DS 1511-1512). It is a sin which will be transmitted by propagation to all mankind, that is, by the transmission of a human nature deprived of original holiness and justice. And that is why original sin is called "sin" only in an analogical sense: it is a sin "contracted" and not "committed" - a state and not an act.

TRANSMISSION OF THE SIN BY GENERATION

Thomas had explained the transmission of original sin by the mechanism of our biological presence in Adam. The *CCC* did not explicitly pick up this biological argument.

Thomas theorized that we were already in Adam when he sinned, therefore we somehow sinned when he did: "Accordingly the original sin of all men was in Adam indeed, as in its principal cause, according to the words of the Apostle (Rom 5:12): 'In whom all have sinned.'" (*ST* III,-83,,1).

But the translation "<u>In</u> <u>whom</u> all have sinned," is probably wrong. It differs from the original Greek of Rom 5:12. Most versions today read: "<u>Because</u> all have sinned." The translation of the Greek <u>eph ho</u> and of the Latin <u>in quo</u> has been the subject of much dispute. If we accept the translation "<u>Because</u> all have sinned" which is more likely the correct one, we remain open to a non-biological explanation. We then explain the inheritance of Adam's sin in a more diffuse sense: "<u>because</u>" Adam sinned.

Thomas had wrestled with the biological concept, which apparently did not satisfy him completely. He therefore blended our biological presence in Adam with a political imputability together with him. He makes this bio-political combo the pathway by which original sin reaches us:

> All men born of Adam may be considered as one man, inasmuch as they have one common nature, which they receive from their first parents; even as in civil matters, all who are members of one community are reputed as one body, and the whole community as one man. Indeed . . . by sharing the same species, many men are one man.' Accordingly the multitude of men born of Adam, are as so many members of one body (*ST* I-II,81,1).

The sin which is in a person born of Adam is voluntary,

states Thomas, not by that individual person's will "but by the will of his first parent, who, by the movement of generation, moves all who originate from him, even as the soul's will moves all the members to their actions" (ibid.; see also *De Malo*, 4,5). Adam, then, sinned in the name of all of us, much as Levi is said to have paid tithes to Melchizedek while still in the loins of Abraham (cf. Heb 7:9). God had constituted Adam as the head of the human race. By raising Adam to the state of supernatural grace, God intended to raise the entire race to that level together with Adam. When Adam lost this grace for himself by sinning, he lost it for his offspring as well. Various wordings of this explanation express the teaching in essentially the same manner (see e.g. Herve, II,433).

This standard explanation appears to imply that God punishes all descendants of Adam for his sin; that He chastises the race for the sin of the first parent. Many are not pleased with this solution; some attempt a more felicitous wording or prefer to leave the matter unexplained.

FURTHER ATTEMPTS TO EXPLAIN THE SIN IN US

What tends to disturb us about the standard explanation is that, somehow, God punishes US for what someone else did; that God punishes me today, for what Adam did yesterday. This is difficult to reconcile with our concept of God's impartial justice. God is absolutely just we know, and does not punish one person for the wrong that another person did. He does not punish children for the sins of their fathers. Ezekiel corrected false notions about God's supposed communal punishments when he insisted strongly that "a son is not to suffer because of his father's sins" (18:20). Likewise Christ corrected His disciples when they asked Him: "Rabbi, who sinned, this man or his parents, that he was born blind?" (Jn 9:2). Christ responded that neither the man nor his parents had caused the blindness by a sin. It was to be an occasion to show forth the works of God.

Yet in the Old Testament we do find references to communal punishment for the sins of individuals. For example: "For I, the Lord your God, am a jealous God, inflicting punishment for their father's wickedness on the children of those who hate me, down to the third and fourth generation; but bestowing mercy down to the thousandth generation" (Ex 20:5; see also, e.g. Deut 5:9; Tob 9:11). We must read this Old Testament concept of communal punishment for sin in its context, however, lest we give it a false interpretation. This description of God is poetic, a symbolic manner of teaching how much greater is God's inclination to have mercy than to punish. Ezekiel explicitly rejected the notion that God punishes children for the sins of their parents.

The concept that children can and do suffer punishment for the sins of their elders is very true to life, however, in another sense. Children do not inherit guilt from their parents, but they do inherit physical defects from them. If during a pregnancy a mother smoked excessively, or indulged in alcohol, or took drugs, the child may inherit physical disabilities by way of chromosomal damage. The poison in the mother's blood stream crosses the threshold of the placenta and affects the child. God is not punishing the child directly for the unhealthy indulgence of the parent, but the child suffers nevertheless from the mother's action. Similarly, if a father gambles away the family income at the race tracks, the children may suffer physically from lack of proper food.

This concept allows us to reason that God does not punish us directly for the sin of Adam. Rather, we are born into a spiritual poorhouse because our first parents gambled away the family inheritance. Such is the gist of the explanation which I will now propose.

DO NOT CAST YOUR PEARLS BEFORE SWINE

"Do not give what is holy to dogs, or toss your pearls before swine" (Mt 7:6) admonished Christ. He made His point starkly clear: "Don't waste precious gifts on unappreciative recipients." Applied to our subject, it interprets the mind of God to say: "I will not give the pearl of grace to members of the human family indiscriminately, without some guarantee that it will be treasured and appreciated." Given the present state of the sinful human race, God would waste His gifts were He to bestow sanctifying grace upon everyone at birth. That would violate principles of good management.

After His Resurrection, Christ appeared to His circle of friends, but kept His distance from enemies. He restricted His appearances to the Faith community. Similarly we can theorize that God now restores Adam's original gifts only to the Faith community. He does not thrust His grace upon the crowd at random, because some prefer to make themselves enemies of God, spurners of His gifts.

The central thought in this is that, with the commission of original sin, God changed His administration for the human race in reference to grace. Before the sin the human race was one united and believing society in paradise. None of the members was ignorant of God, none was an enemy of Him. By definition the entire race was initially obedient to the Creator and Father. God's plan to constitute the children of Adam and Eve in the same state of holiness and justice as He had constituted the parents would have been wise and reasonable before the sin. His grace would be welcomed and treasured in the believing community.

After the sin the human family is no longer a community which preserves and guarantees communal obedience to God. Some people of this disunited scattering of humans spread out over the globe believe in Him, others do not, still others reject Him outright. The All-wise God no longer sees His way clear to bestow grace upon each person when He creates him. So He changed administrative methods: God now bestows grace only upon those humans who ask for it; those who seek it by way of established norms, either personally or through their parents or guardians. Christ has established Baptism as the normal channel through which He bestows the gift of grace. Baptism is understood here in its broad meaning, including Baptism by water, by desire, and by martyrdom. That includes all who accept God's friendship in the manner which God alone may know.

In this proposed explanation, God does not endow humans with grace automatically for the same reason as the Church legislates conditions for the reception of the Sacrament of Baptism. She withholds Baptism from children if there is not even a minimum of assurance that they will be educated in the truths and commandments of Faith. This norm of the Church is reflected in Canon 868:

Canon 868: For the licit baptism of an infant it is

necessary that ... there be a founded hope that the infant will be brought up in the Catholic religion; if such hope is altogether lacking, the baptism is to be put off according to the prescriptions of particular law and the parents are to be informed of the reason.

Before Adam committed original sin, his family -- which was the world family -- gave reasonable assurance that the descendants would be educated in the revealed religion. Into that world family God could wisely give the gift of grace to each child when He created it. The community would educate that child to cherish the gift of grace.

All that changed when Adam sinned. After original sin God no longer receives assurance that the human community will educate every newborn child to live and persevere in the state of sinlessness, of holiness and justice. It is not proper for God to toss pearls of grace to all humans in a non-discriminating manner with eyes closed to realitiies. Some recipients of grace in the fallen community might not care for it, might neglect it, might even repudiate it. Some parents would not care to educate their children religiously even should God coerce His grace upon all.

In the original Eden grace was to flow to each new person by way of propagation. The parents and community would educate each new member properly. So long as racial solidarity remained firmly committed to pursue holiness and justice as an uncompromising and compactual community policy, God could then lovingly provide the gift of grace to each new member of the race at the moment of conception. Such was the atmosphere in Eden before original sin.

Original sin shattered that virginal solidarity. God now waits for parents to come forward voluntarily to request the gift for their children. An Apostolic Tradition of infant Baptism, reflecting the will of Christ, directs believing parents to present their children to the font of Baptism. He waits also for adult individuals to come forward of their own accord. God is not a foolish spendthrift who scatters the precious gift of sanctifying grace broadside over the world without looking whether a field is cultivated to make His seed grow.

THE "SIN OF THE WORLD" THWARTS GOD'S PLAN

This explanation does not claim that God punishes the race or individuals for an original sin of Adam. Rather the human community itself, yesterday and today, does not obey God as it ought; does not commit itself individually and in racial solidarity, privately and publicly, with whole heart and soul and mind and strength, to our supernatural calling. We, individually and socially, in our private lives and in the public sphere, neglect to carry out a total commitment to live in accordance with God's call to live here as His creatures ought to live, in preparation for life hereafter in heaven. We fail individually by sinning in our private lives, and we fail to work in solidarity to shape our public institutions in a manner which facilitates an understanding of our moral obligations, and motivates each and all to use the means God provides to carry them out. God provides us with all we need to move back into Eden, on condition that we are willing to do so. The means He provides so generously are not only the natural faculties which are inadequate for the supernatural calling -- though the Pelagian Heresy denied this; God also provides ample supernatural helps: revelation, grace, the Sacraments, the teaching and guiding Church. What is lacking is a receptive atmosphere which would enable God, without acting foolishly, to entrust grace to each new member who enters that community. It is not God, then, who punishes the community for original sin. It is the community itself which, by its sinful state, by its "sin of the world" as some call it, dis-invites God from bestowing His gift on all new members of the race automatically.

This "sin of the world" is an unbroken continuation of the original transgression of our Adam and Eve. The <u>originating</u> sin occasioned the spawning of <u>originated</u> <u>sin</u> in which the world now languors. The world punishes itself by refusing to adopt a global lifestyle compatible with solidarity in grace. This lack of human solidarity in grace is the feedback to God which thrusts upon Him the logical necessity to allow the reign of original sin to continue.

But far from punishing the babies, God bestows grace on them just as soon as their parents bring them to the baptismal font. God is always ready, is always on call, is eager to respond to our search for grace. He will come quickly to each one's door to deliver His gift. He then makes the shadow of original sin disappear from the soul and emblazons the person with the radiant splendor of sanctifying grace. Happily, parents can extract themselves and their children from this catastrophic deprivation by means of Baptism.

This theory illumines the reason for the existence of original sin without implying that God is unjust in some manner. It also by-passes the explanation of Thomas that we all sinned in Adam because we were in his loins biologically. It turns the blame on ourselves, not so much on Adam. We ourselves are doing the sinning today which perpetuates the situation once begun by Adam.

THE NATURE OF ORIGINAL SIN IN US

God originally called our first parents to think and act as He does insofar as this is possible to supernaturally capacitated creatures. He adopted Adam and Eve into His private family. If they persevere, He will admit them into His presence in heaven. Christ referred to this mysterious reality, which transcends sense perceptions and powers of observation, in His High Priestly Prayer:

> And this is eternal life, that they may know you, the only true God, and Jesus Christ whom you have sent...As you, Father, are in me and I am in you, may they also be in us...The glory that you have given me I have given them, so that they may be one, as we are one, I in them and you in me, that they may become completely one. Father, I desire that those also, whom you have given me, may be with me where I am, to see my glory, which you have given me because you loved me before the foundation of the world" (Jn 17).

The proper response to an invitation made by God to become adopted members of His family is gratitude and joyful acceptance. God initially invited every descendant of Adam to this adoption into the divine family through the original grace He gave to Adam. This invitation continues even now, and is valid despite the by-gone rejection by Adam. It is a standing call from God to all the children of Adam to enter the intimate life of the Trinity, the cause for which Christ offered His High Priestly Prayer.

Though called, children cannot respond to that call of their own accord at the time of childhood because they cannot perceive the call. Only if their parents or guardians bring them to Baptism can they become obedient to God's call and invitation. If their parents do not bring them to Baptism, they are situated, unbeknown to themselves, in a static stand-off of disobedience against God. They ought to respond positively to God's communications, but, like autistic children, remain dumb and uncomprehending.

God is not pleased when, because of neglect of the parents, children are not baptized. Nor is He satisfied when the human race does not cultivate an environment completely receptive to grace. Our morally chaotic world prevents Him from endowing every new child with grace automatically at the time when He creates that new person. That God is not pleased with this persistent and stiff necked "sin situation," which distances people from Him, is illustrated by Christ's parable about the wedding feast:

> The kingdom of heaven may be compared to a king who gave a wedding banquet for his son. He sent his slaves to call those who had been invited to the wedding banquet, but they would not come....The king was enraged (Mt 22:2-3,7).

Objective disobedience against God's invitation to live a life in supernatural grace is the state in which we are born. This disobedience is not rectified for infants until parents bring them to the font; nor for adults until they freely receive Baptism, whether of water, or desire, or blood. The objective and overt disobedience of the corporate earthly population is not rectified until the race converts; until individuals, families, governments, the United Nations, the entire human race, profess the Credo and live it unerringly. Until that is done we continue the corporate racial rebellion now still in force so many years after Adam and Eve started it.

Another aspect of original sin in us is our birth into a situation of rebellion against God. Being without grace at birth, we belong to Adam who had lost grace by sin, but had not yet regained it by repentance. We are stillborn into the moment of Adam's spiritual death of soul. The Bible implies that our first parents converted from their sin of rebellion when they responded to God's call in the garden of Eden. Even though they confessed their sin reluctantly, making excuses, the Bible states that they did confess it. They also accepted their penance, however reluctantly. God then clothed them in leather garments which signifies their conversion and renewed friendship (see Genesis 3). We are not born, however, into the situation of their renewed friendship with God. We enter the world of their previous moment of rebellion. We are stripped of grace when born.

We are also born into the camp of God's sworn enemy: into the camp of the crafty serpent which crawled out of paradise on its belly but only after it had done its wicked work. Unless we rectify this situation of objective rebellion by receiving Baptism, we remain unconverted and separated from God, dead in soul, unanimated by supernatural life, and somehow subjected to the conquest of the serpent.

THE SIN: UNDONE BY EXORCISM AND BAPTISM

The Church exorcises the Devil out of infants before pouring the waters of Baptism. Original sin kidnaps us into "the power of ... the devil" (cf. Council Trent, Canon 1 on original sin, DS 1511). The Church is now the woman who is at enmity with the ancient serpent. "Do you renounce Satan?" asks the Church of the child. The sponsors answer for it: "I do." Satan has to go. The Church stands tall and commands the Devil to depart forthwith from this child. Having rid the child of the serpent's pretentious claim, the priest then pours the waters: "Child, I baptize you in the name of the Father, and of the Son, and of the Holy Spirit."

Then occurs that for which Christ prayed at the Last Supper: "That the love with which you have loved me may be in this child and that I, Christ, may live in it" (cf. Jn 17:26). The child is thereby adopted into God's family with a title to enter heaven at the time of departure from this life. It has only to bring along its white garment, either unsullied by sin, or laundered and restored after sin.

Pope Leo the Great, in one of his monumental sermons on Christ's Passion, tells us that Christ undoes the harm that Adam had done for us; that we are a new people in Christ now; that we can proudly stride right back into to the paradise from which Adam had been ousted:

> Ignorance has been destroyed, obstinacy has been overcome. The sacred blood of Christ has quenched the flaming sword that barred access to the tree of life. The age-old night of sin has given place to the true light.

The Christian people are invited to share the riches of paradise. All who have been reborn have the way open before them to return to their native land, from which they had been exiled. Unless they indeed close off for themselves the path that could be opened before the faith of a thief (Sermo 15, De Passione Domini, 3-4 PL 54, 366-367; in *Liturgy of the Hours*, Thursday, Fourth Week of Lent).

Chapter 12

IRENAEUS ON ORIGINAL SIN

The writings of St. Irenaeus (c.125-c.202) on original sin are implacably optimistic, contrasting remarkably from those of St. Augustine (354-430). He is also closer in time to the final deposition of the Apostolic Tradition: Christ taught the Apostles, who educated Polycarp, who instructed Irenaeus. We therefore have a very early witness to the Tradition of the Apostles in the writings of St. Irenaeus.

Irenaeus was not a polished rhetorician like Augustine. When asking indulgence from his readers, he explains that he was born in Greek-speaking Smyrna of Asia Minor, but he did not live and work in academe. He spent his life in frontier Lyons where he spoke to peasants in their native tongue. But we will experience that his thoughts are lofty, his heart is warm, his memory is sharp, and his learning is prodigious. His five-volume book *Adversus Haereses* written in Greek took to task the pseudo-science of sophisticated gnostics of his day and nailed them to the wall.

Irenaeus and Augustine teach in agreement that Adam sinned and lost his initial endowment of friendship with God, and that all people die as a result of Adam's sin. But whereas Augustine sees God's pristine plans frustrated by original sin, Irenaeus sees the same sin as an almost necessary step for the education of mankind. Irenaeus sees God laying out His plans with original sin already foreseen from the beginning. He would create man free, He foresaw the sin, He then made provisions accordingly. He would help man how to use that freedom properly, with original sin as a stepping stone to facilitate the learning process.

Christ would come fully prepared to cope with the situation of the fallen race. He would recapitulate the fallen race and lead it to the Father.

Augustine, however, would project Christ as an afterthought - as a second plan after the first had failed. Christ is sent into the world as a Repairman, to patch up the disaster caused by Adam. Even so, Augustine has us living in a world not completely repaired by Christ. It is a world, he maintains, in which God still punishes us for Adam's misdeed. It is as though we live in the suburbs of Chernoble after the nuclear meltdown.

ST. IRENAEUS, FOUNDER OF CHRISTIAN THEOLOGY

Irenaeus came from Greek-speaking Smyrna of Asia Minor, where he inherited oriental theology concerning original sin, insofar as such theology had been developed. In his youth he learned doctrine at the feet of his bishop, the future martyr St. Polycarp (c.69-c.155). Scarcely a hundred miles from Smyrna was Ephesus, reportedly the home of Mary and St. John. John was never far from Mary, Polycarp was never far from John, and Irenaeus sat at the feet of Polycarp to learn the Apostolic Tradition at its primeval source. He writes about it to the Roman presbyter Florinus:

> For, when I was still a boy, I knew you (Florinus) in lower Asia, in Polycarp's house...I remember the events of those days more clearly than those which happened recently...how he (Polycarp) sat and disputed,...how he reported his intercourse with John and with the others who had seen the Lord, how he remembered their words, and what

were the things concerning the Lord which he had heard from them, and how Polycarp had received them from the eye-witnesses of the Word of Life, and reported all things in agreement with the Scriptures. I listened eagerly even then to these things ...and made notes of them, not on paper, but in my heart, and ever by the grace of God do I truly ruminate on them (*Euseb. History of the Church* 5:20,5-7; trans. by Johannes Quasten, *Patrology* I,287).

The witness of Irenaeus to the Gospel is therefore priceless. He moved from Smyrna to France where he served as a priest at Lyons, whose parishioners esteemed him highly. While he was away at Rome in 177, a persecution broke out in Lyons during which its bishop, St. Pothinus, was martyred. Upon the return of Irenaeus he was made Bishop of Lyons around the year 178. From his writings we get a privileged view of teachings about original sin being circulated in the early Church.

A few letters of Irenaeus have survived the centuries, but the two great works for which he is called the "Founder of Christian Theology" are the book *Proof of the Apostolic Preaching* (hereafter referred to as *Proof*), and the five-volume set called *Adversus Haereses* (hereafter referred to by book, chapter, and paragraph, e.g. III,22,8). He wrote in the Greek language, but the original versions are lost; the *Proof* is preserved in an Armenian translation, and the *Adv. Haer.* in Latin (cf. Johannes Quasten, *Patrology* I, 290). This latter work was so convincing that it practically gave the <u>coup de grace</u> to the seething and very popular Gnostic heresies fermenting among dilettante Christians in much of the Mediterranean Basin of his day - not entirely unlike the new age yeast fermenting in America today.

Irenaeus took special pride in giving witness to the Tradition handed down by the apostles (cf. III,3,3). He writes with charm, sometimes with humor, but hardly with elegance of letters, for which he asks our understanding. The busy bishop wrote over the span of decades, sometimes repeating, sometimes nuancing teachings for different audiences in a manner which is not always consistent with what he had written long before.

This early Father of the Church quotes the Gospels and Epistles, the Old Testament and the New, to build up his arguments. Likely he quotes routinely from a source which we no longer possess, which was a kind of notebook for teachers of the faith, "a collection of texts under argument-headings" (see J.A. Smith, 33). The Canon of the New Testament had not yet been finalized, but he freely quotes as Scripture from books which would later become a formal part of the books of the New Testament.

CHRIST, RE-CAPITULATOR OF THE COSMOS

Christ's role as re-capitulator of the human race through His Incarnation and Redemption forms the core of Irenaean theology. The Saint of Lyons identifies the Second Person of the Blessed Trinity as the one who deals with mankind in the Old Testament even before His Incarnation. Indeed it is the Son of God who creatively designed the universe, who tailored it to be a fitting environment for His future habitation. The thought is in accord with Hebrews, where the Father addresses this profoundly significant witness to Christ as Founder of the cosmos: "Thou, Lord, didst found the earth in the beginning, and the heavens are the work of thy hands" (Heb 1:10). St. Irenaeus follows through with the insight that Christ is not only Creator of the universe, but is also its <u>raison</u> d'etre, the reason for its creation in the first place. All lines of the cosmos therefore focus on Christ. Christ is not an afterthought conceived in God's mind as a response to the sin of Adam; on the contrary, Christ is the Alpha and Omega of the cosmos in the first place; Adam is fitted into the cosmic plans as the strategic gateway through which Christ will enter it:

> He recapitulates in Himself all the nations dispersed since Adam, and all the languages and generations of men, including Adam himself. That is why St. Paul calls Adam the "type of the One who was to come" (cf. Rom 5:14), because the Word, the maker of all things, did a preliminary sketch in Adam of what, in God's plan, was to come to the human race through the Son of God. God arranged it so that the first man was animal in nature and saved by the spiritual Man. Since the Savior existed already, the one to be saved had to be brought into existence, so that the Saviour should not be in vain (*Adv. Haer.* III,22,3; trans. by John Saward, 64).

Note this singular and exceedingly meaningful final sentence. It makes Adam into a "front man" to pave the way for the main event, the arrival of Christ. Irenaeus presents Christ as the towering and dominant figure who is central to divine planning. Christ, Pantokrator, is the focal point in God's design of the cosmos to be created, the central figure for whom God measures the layout of the universe. The saint of Lyons looks to Christ as the keystone of the cosmos, whereas Adam enters it secondarily in the train of logic following Christ, "so that the Saviour should not be in vain." Adam is created to provide Christ with a worthy cause to activate His great love. In Latin this extraordinary sentence reads: <u>Cum</u> <u>enim</u> <u>praeexisteret</u> <u>salvans,</u> <u>opportebat</u> <u>et</u> <u>quod</u> <u>salvaretur</u> <u>fieri,</u> <u>uti</u> <u>non</u> <u>vacuum</u> <u>sit</u> <u>salvans.</u> Adam is ushered in to become the beneficiary of Christ's work of love.

Here the thought of Irenaeus differs from that of Augustine and Thomas. Irenaeus sees Christ before he finds Adam. Christ is the dominating cosmic King, Adam is a service pawn. Whereas Augustine and Thomas see Adam before they see Christ. Adam, by his sin, occasions a change in God's original plans, namely the sending of Christ into the cosmos. Thomas tends to agree with Augustine whom he quotes: "Augustine says (<u>De</u> <u>Verb.</u> <u>Apost.</u> 8,2) '...Therefore if man had not sinned, the Son of Man would not have come'" *Summa Theologica* III, 1,3). In other words, God decreed the Incarnation of Christ <u>in</u> <u>response</u> to the sin of Adam, to save the situation after Adam had spoiled God's <u>first</u> plan by committing original sin. Not so Irenaeus, who presents Christ as the dominant figure, indeed the <u>raison</u> <u>d'etre,</u> of all creation. Adam is secondary in God's plans, as the subject whom God creates for Christ to sanctify. God, so reasons Irenaeus, had scripted Christ's function as the central focus of the cosmos before taking original sin into divine accounting. Duns Scotus (d.1308) would later develop this remarkable theme of Irenaeus more fully.

The word <u>salvans</u> (the one who saves) which Irenaeus uses to designate Christ's role, does not have the narrow meaning of a Savior who merely pays a ransom to rescue sinners. The word <u>Savior</u> means to Irenaeus, and to the

Greek Fathers typically, the more inclusive role of Sanctifier. The Sanctifier elevates the natural man to the supernatural state originally, as well as after the Fall. Christ, in the
concept of Irenaeus, elevated Adam to the state of holiness and justice before the Fall, and redeemed him after it.
He is more than a repair-man who reconditions a damaged
product. He is an architect who builds the structure originally according to God's primal plan, and then reconditions
it even more magnificently after Adam's temporary crash.

AUGUSTINIAN PESSIMISM VS. IRENAEAN OPTIMISM

Augustine and Irenaeus read the same Genesis Chapters 2-
3, but for Augustine original sin was a disaster repaired
only partially by Christ. Whereas for Irenaeus the sin was
more like the first fall of a baby just learning to walk.
Theologian Denis Minns, OP, contrasts the view of the two
as follows:

> Augustine read the story (of Genesis) in a much
> more literal way (than Irenaeus). The story of the
> sin of Adam and his punishment and death was,
> for him, a story of the past, but all human beings,
> as the progeny of Adam, were enmeshed in that
> past. Although Adam's sin has continuing and
> appalling consequences for all the descendants of
> Adam, there is nothing these descendants can do
> about it. All the action happened in the first chap-
> ter of the story of humankind and the subsequent
> chapters have to do with the ineluctable unfolding
> of the consequences of that action (Minns, *Iren-
> aeus*, 58).

For Augustine, Adam's action sealed the fate of much of

mankind. Not so for Irenaeus, who lived closer to the time of Christ and of the Apostles. For Irenaeus, Christ takes into Himself all of mankind, including Adam, and makes His redemptive action extend to the entire human race. Minns continues his analysis:

> This is in the strongest contrast to Irenaeus's understanding, because, for him, the history of humankind and the history of salvation are one and the same. This path may twist and wander through many detours, but there is no radical bifurcation...The human race was predestined in Adam, but it was predestined to come to be in the image and likeness of God (Minns, 58-59).

PARADISE AND ORIGINAL SIN

The work of Irenaeus called *Proof of the Apostolic Preaching* begins with a capsulized but magnificent and endearing version of creation and the Fall. The English translation is that of J.P. Smith, S.J.:

> But man He fashioned with His own hands, taking of the purest and finest of earth, in measured wise mingling with the earth His own power; for He gave his frame the outline of His own form, that the visible appearance too should be godlike - for it was an image of God that man was fashioned and set on earth - and that he might come to life, He breathed into his face the breath of life, so that the man become like God in inspiration as well as in frame... (*Proof*,11).

Note the special care of God in fashioning the human body

and soul: He made the <u>body</u> "godlike" in <u>appearance</u>, and
the <u>soul</u> "godlike" in <u>inspiration</u>. In Irenaeus, all that God
does is beautiful. The shape of the body itself is "godlike"
he observed, admiring its beauty. Even more so is the soul
godlike. It is the breath of life which God insufflated into
the body. The breath is an image of God. It is durable, it is
immortal, it lives forever (cf.II,34,4). This <u>anima</u>, endowed
with intellect and free will, will never cease to live once
God has brought it into being. The image of God is like
God insofar as it has no end and will live forever. But it is
unlike God insofar as God has no beginning, but the <u>anima</u>
has a beginning.

The "likeness" to God imprinted into this <u>anima,</u> however,
is not its substance. It is an endowment which can be
eradicated from the <u>anima</u> by sin. But even after sin, the
Spirit can restore the likeness once again (cf. V,6,1).
Obviously Irenaeus was a skilled teacher, clarifying for the
neo-christians, who were troubled by gnostic errors, a
basic truth: sin affects adversely the spiritual beauty of the
soul and destroys the image of God which grace builds up
in it. But all is not lost when one sins, because the Spirit
can restore one to the original glory.

Irenaeus plays out this theme of grace: it can enter the
soul, can leave it by reason of sin, and then enter again.
The "likeness" is God's breath given by the Spirit: "The
Spirit has formed man to the likeness of God" (*Proof*, No.
5, see Smith p. 50). When man loses the image through
sin, the Spirit can restore it again.

THE WORD OF GOD WALKS WITH ADAM IN PARADISE

Irenaeus paints an idyllic picture of the pristine paradise.

He may have used a common catechetical aid in circulation at the time. Life in paradise was lovely before the sin. God had prepared the Garden for Adam, in which the animals were already grown, but Adam and Eve were still children. Irenaeus typically identifies the "Word of God" as the One who walks in Paradise with our first parents, "prefiguring" His future Incarnation.

> And so fair and goodly was the Garden, the Word of God was constantly walking in it; He would walk around and talk with the man, prefiguring what was to come to pass in the future, how He would become man's fellow, and talk with him, and come among mankind teaching them justice (*Proof*, 12).

PRIMAL INNOCENCE

"Why did Adam lose his primal innocence so easily?" asks Irenaeus. He explains that Adam did not yet have the advantage of possessing the clear kind of knowledge that we now possess ever since Christ became Incarnate to be our Teacher:

> For in times past it was <u>said</u> that man was made in the image of God, but not <u>shown</u>, because the Word in whose image man was made, was still invisible. That is why man lost the likeness so easily. But when the Word of God was made flesh, He confirmed both things: He showed the true image, when He Himself became what His image was; and He restored and made fast the likeness, making man like the invisible Father through the visible Word" (V,16,2; trans. Saward).

Furthermore, argues Irenaeus, Adam and Eve fell into the temptation easily by reason of inexperience. They had been freshly formed from the clay, and their thoughts were like those of children. They had not yet gained the wisdom which can be acquired through testing: "But the man was a little one, and his discretion still undeveloped, wherefore also he was easily misled by the deceiver"...(Proof, 12). A special feature of Irenaean theology is that he regards Adam and Eve before their Fall as children still in their latent years in regard to sexual development:

> And Adam and Eve (for this is the name of the woman) were naked and were not ashamed, for their thoughts were innocent and childlike, and they had no conception or imagination of the sort that is engendered in the soul by evil through con-cupiscence, and by lust. For they were then in their integrity, preserving their natural state, for what had been breathed into their frame was the spirit of life; now, so long as the spirit still remains in proper order and vigour, it is without imagination or conception of what is shameful. For this reason they were not ashamed, as they kissed each other and embraced with the innocence of childhood (*Proof*, 14).

The concept that Adam and Eve were still children when they sinned was commonly accepted by some of the Fathers at the time of Irenaeus. "In accordance with the idea that Adam was created for development, we find in Theo-philus [sixth bishop of Antioch] the fancy, which spread to other Fathers, that the first parents of the race were but 'infants' in age at the time of their transgression. Their sin was associated with the desire to become wise beyond their years: 'And at the same time He wished man, infant as he was, to remain for some time longer simple and sincere (II,25)'" (Tennant,282). Clement of Alexandria likewise calls Adam a "boy" (*Paidion tou Theou*) before his fall, and adds that with the sin he became a man (*Ho pais andrizomenos apeitheia (Protr.* II.III.I, see J.P. Smith, 150).

That the man was a "little one" whose discretion was still undeveloped is a notion which can be disputed from the biblical context. But this is genuine Irenaeus. For example:

> Because they had been created but a short time before, they had no knowledge about generating children; they first had to grow up and from that time on multiply in this manner" (III,22).

Irenaeus by no means presents Adam in paradise as a superman of unmatched intelligence. E.R. Tennant, who made an exhaustive study of the sources of doctrine on original sin, rightly points out that Irenaeus considers Adam in paradise to be still a child at the onset of development, both natural and supernatural (cf. Tennant, 285). He described Adam as an "infant" (IV,38.1) whom God did not miraculously make wise nor holy beyond the range of his tender age. God did not create Adam and Eve as adults, but as children. They could not manage to think and act as adults initially, because they had not yet become of age: "God had the power at the beginning to grant perfection to man; but as the latter (Adam) was only recently created, he could not possibly have received it...or retained it" (IV,38.2). The Irenaean Adam, then, is not like an angel in paradise, is not a miracle man into whom God infused wisdom surpassing his age. Irenaeus pictures the event of original sin as a shock which accelerated development in both areas, the natural and the supernatural.

Christ takes Adam from where he is, fallen from grace and still inexperienced. He nurtures him from the lost innocence of childhood into spiritual adulthood. He forgives Adam and Eve their first sin, and then helps them to achieve holiness. Christ is Adam's Pedagogue and Model.

Ancient Jewish writings had ascribed to our first parents in paradise exceedingly extraordinary celestial privileges (Tennant, 330). Their influence doubtless trickled down to St. Augustine who then made this concept a standard fixture of doctrine on original sin. Ambrose, mentor of St. Augustine, had made Adam almost an angel: "His life was similar to that of the angels" (*De Parad.* 42). Who, when he sinned, "put away his heavenly image and assumed an earthly form" (*sed ubi lapsus est, deposuit imaginem coelestis, sumsit terrestris effigiem; Hexaemer.* 6,7; see Tennant, 339). If St. Irenaeus knew about this notion of a superman Adam before the Fall, he does not mention it. He gives quite a contrary picture of an uninitiated Adam as still a child who possessed only limited intellectual and moral capabilities. We legitimately draw the conclusion from this that there was no Tradition taught by the Apostles that Adam in paradise was a superman with intelligence like that of the angels. This was not a doctrine taught by Christ nor the Apostles. Rather it was an invention of theologians who spoke from personal conviction.

St. Irenaeus, hammering away at heretics who exalted Adam as a celestial being, took delight in reminding them again and again that Adam was made of mud. He had lowly beginnings. God wanted it to be so, for He preferred that humans develop virtue by exerting themselves rather than to be initially invested with pre-fabricated virtue. "The notion that Adam was not created perfect, but rather... intended to come to be in the likeness of God at the end of a process of development, is Irenaeus' most characteristic understanding of Genesis 1:26, and the one that most coheres with the rest of his theological scheme" (Minns, 61; see *Ad. Her.* V, 16,2). Irenaean theology states and assumes that Adam was weak in the beginning, with no more knowledge than a child or an adolescent. He needed time, he needed experience, to grow to maturity. "Humankind needed to grow accustomed to bearing divinity" through trial and gradual maturation (Minns, 61, *Ad. Her.* III,20,2). Irenaeus purposely took the heretics to task for their assumption that God created Adam as a superman with towering intellect and strong will-power.

We ask ourselves now, is Augustine correct when he interprets "naked without shame" as an indication that Adam had motor control over the passions? Or is Irenaeus correct when he interprets the same words to indicate that Adam was still a child in the years of sexual latency? Irenaeus heard from Polycarp what the Apostles had taught. Augustine lived several centuries later. Very likely, then, there is no Apostolic Tradition which would affirm Augustine over Irenaeus on this point. This indicates that we have no certainty from Apostolic Tradition that Adam was without concupiscence before the Fall; and from the same Tradition we have no certainty that original sin somehow altered our bodies, our passions, our drives; in consequence, there is no sure witness from this source that original sin has made our natures more prone to sin now than in the situation before the Fall, after we recover the state of grace. That is, unless and until the Magisterium of the Church finds it to be a part of her living Tradition.

Chapter 13

PIONEER THEOLOGY OF IRENAEUS

ADAM AND EVE HAD REAL BODIES

On the one hand Irenaeus hammered away at the heretics by insisting that Adam was not a celestial being of angelic nature; he was a man of lowly origin. The life of Adam began when God took mud and fashioned it into a body. On the other hand, this body, male and female, is not a despicable, depraved, evil object attached to human souls. It is a noble creation fashioned and modelled after the pattern of Christ's body. In and through the body humans give glory to God. When gnostics extolled the soul as of higher origin than the body, and discounted the body as evil in origin, this fired Irenaeus to remind them that <u>we are body</u>, that God made humanity from earth:

> The high "spirituality" of his opponents provoked distrust in Irenaeus. It also seems to have heightened his own delight in the material, fleshly dimensions of the human condition which so disgusted them. At every opportunity, he provocatively reminds them that the first human being was made from earth. When the gnostics say that real human beings are spiritual and lightsome he insists they are nothing of the sort: they are, indeed, profoundly material and earthy, they are made of mud (Minns, 57).

In agreement with his notion of the beauty and nobility of the human body, Irenaeus does not assign to Adam's maleness a special theological significance. He symbolizes all humanity, male and female. He assigns to Eve a significance parallel to Adam in this respect. She is the mother of all the living. Later Christian tradition makes the maleness of Adam of special theological significance, but not so Irenaeus. All humanity simply began with the mud from which God formed humankind. From this humble beginning issues Adam and Eve, issues Mary and Christ. For Irenaeus the Virgin Mary also represents humanity rather than womanhood. "For she, and she alone, is the guarantor of Christ's humanity; Christ is a human being (<u>anthropos</u>) because he derives his flesh from the first human being (<u>anthropos</u>) by way of the human being (<u>anthropos</u>) who is his mother" (Minns, 58, <u>Ad</u>. <u>Her</u>. III,19,3; 23,1.) Minns notes that although <u>anthropos</u> is a noun of masculine gender, it is given a feminine article when an author intends to designate a human being of the female sex. The Latin translation in this case makes it clear that Irenaeus describes Mary as an <u>anthropos</u>, a member of stream of humanity whose beginnings God fashioned from mud.

THE FALL FROM GRACE

The saint relates how God put Adam and Eve to the test; they should freely demonstrate in action that they acknowledge their dependence upon Him. If they obey they need not die, and they can remain in this extraordinary Garden which differs so wonderfully from the world outside. Unfortunately, they did not pass the test, became mortal, and had to face hardships outside of Eden:

> Expelled from the Garden, Adam and his wife Eve fell into many miseries of mind and body, walking in this world with sadness and toil and sighs... (*Proof*, pp. 54, 57; trans. of Joseph P. Smith, slightly modified.

The saint of Lyons definitely attributes to innocent Adam and Eve a special mode of spiritual life which would be theirs so long as they did not disobey God, so long as "the spirit still remains in proper order and vigour." The Council of Trent would later refer to their state as one of holiness and justice. Pope John Paul II did not hesitate to call this spiritual mode by the current theological term "sanctifying grace" (General Audience 3 September 1986).

The fact that Irenaeus characterizes Adam and Eve before the Fall as friends of God, as walking and conversing with Him, as possessing His image and likeness, shows that he regards them as civilized and cultured people. He would not at all agree with the contention of some evolutionists who depict our first humans as dimwitted dawn people, newly emerged from the animal world, uncertain about polytheism or monotheism, about monogamy and the "Ten Commandments." Irenaeus considers them to be believing and loving people, adopted children of God, with whom God conversed about theological matters. Irenaeus would not disagree with Sirach who testified: "Above every other created living being was Adam" (Sir 49:16).

ADAM OUR MODEL FOR SPIRITUAL GROWTH

Irenaeus (III,23) has the Divine Word treating Adam and Eve with pity after their sin. The Good Shepherd seeks them out specially because they need Him now more than ever. He observes that God the Word felt concern for the first humans He had made, who would also be His own ancestors. Because He was determined to redeem the human race, it was only right that He begin with the first humans He had created. The One who rescued the race from the enemy should first of all save those who were the first victims of that enemy, who were hurt so badly by it. For the God who came to the aid of man and restored him is not a weak God nor unjust.

The Word, observes Irenaeus, did not curse Adam the person, but the earth. The man had to work hard thereafter, to earn bread with the sweat of his brow, and the woman had to undergo various hardships. In this way God reprimanded them for what they had done in order to bring them to sober repentance and a better way of life, but did not curse them. He cursed the wicked serpent who had deliberately tempted them. He also cursed Cain who refused to repent. But He did not curse Adam and Eve, His ancestors, who repented of their sin (cf. III,23).

After Adam had been seduced, continues Irenaeus, he repented immediately as is shown by his fear of God. He was ashamed to meet God and to speak with Him. Now we know that the beginning of wisdom is the fear of the Lord (Ps 110,10). Recognizing his sin he did penance, and we know that God bestows His kindness upon those who are penitent. Adam could have covered his body with other leaves painless to the body, but he purposely used prickly fig leaves to do well-deserved penance for his disobedience. He was sorry now, fearful of God.

He used the covering of fig leaves likewise to check the wanton onslaught of the flesh, continues Irenaeus. For now he had lost the characteristics of childhood, for thoughts of evil pressed upon him. Fearing God whom he was expecting to meet he contrived this protection of continence for himself and his wife. He meant to express in this way what had happened: "For," he said to himself, "by disobedience I lost the stole of that holiness which I had from the Spirit, and I recognize now that I deserve such a garment, which provides no pleasure but bites and stings the body" (III,23,5). He would have worn this fig leaf covering forever, humbling himself, had not God, who is merciful, clothed them with skins to replace the fig leaf coverings.

God then banned Adam from paradise and so closed off access to the Tree of Life, thus exposing him to the ordinary laws of mortality, continues Irenaeus. God appointed the Virgin and her offspring, he adds, to overpower the ancient serpent, the dragon and anti-Christ, to bind it and crush all its power. For Adam had been conquered by it, and robbed of his whole life. Therefore, when the enemy was conquered in turn, Adam received life again. "For the last enemy to be destroyed is death (1 Cor 15:26). That could not be written truthfully unless the man who was first overcome by death would be freed from it. His salvation, then, is the emptying of death" (III 23,7). Death was then emptied when the Lord gave life to man, that is, to Adam. Irenaeus closes the section with the challenge: "But those who deny salvation to Adam gain nothing by this except that they make themselves to be heretics and apostates from the truth, and show that they are advocates of the serpent and of death" (III,23,8).

ORIGINAL SIN, AN OCCASION FOR GROWTH

Pope John Paul II, in his message to priests for Holy Thursday 1998, encouraged them to grow toward spiritual perfection step by step. The priest is well aware, he said, that he faces "a long crossing on little boats," and that he soars heavenwards "on little wings" (St. Gregory of Nanzianzus, *Theological Poems, 1*).

This echoes the message of Irenaeus that we, like Adam, are expected to acquire perfection by degrees, patiently, and with effort. In Chapter 38 of Book III Irenaeus returns to the point that God did not make Adam perfect initially because at first he was still a child (<u>infans</u> <u>enim</u> <u>fuit</u>). He began as a child and was expected to grow one step at a time into a more and more perfect likeness of the uncreated God (cf. Smith, note 70, p. 150). To embark upon the path of growth he needed to be challenged.

In Chapter 39 Irenaeus then chides us all for wanting to have instant perfection prematurely, instead of growing up gradually under the creative activity of God. We do well to remember, he admonishes, that it is not we who make God, but God who makes us: "It is not you who makes God; God made you!" (III,39,1).

The Bishop of Lyons thus urges all sinners who have fallen like Adam and Eve to recognize that they need the grace of God to rise again. Let them learn from the sad experience of sin, and progress more wisely and patiently in virtue. The words are for all sinners who awaken from the dream of a childlike Adam to the realities of life. Irenaeus presents Adam and Eve as models who pioneered for us the way back to God and to peace of soul.

It is not reasonable, chides Irenaeus, when people refuse to await growth in virtue, and are impatient with themselves, even ascribing their weakness to God. They are ungrateful, unwilling to be what God made them to be, weak at the outset. They want to be instantly perfect, to be like God, to abolish the difference between Him and themselves as creatures (cf. IV, 38,4-5). By His foreknowledge God knew the frailty of man and what would be the result of that weakness. The person who has learned now about good and evil ought to rise to a wiser manner of life:

It is an evil thing not to obey God. That is the death of man. Through the magnanimity which God gave him, man has known both the good of obedience and the evil of disobedience, so that the eye of his mind, having experienced both, might with discernment choose the better, and be neither slothful nor neglectful of the commandment of God. He learns from experience that disobeying God, which robs him of life, is evil, and so he never attempts it... But how would he have discerned the good without knowing its opposite? For first-hand experience is more certain and reliable than conjecture... The mind acquires the knowledge of the good through the experience of both, and becomes more firmly committed to preserving it by obeying God. First, by penance, he rejects disobedience, because it is bitter and evil. Then he realizes what it really is - the opposite of goodness and sweetness, and so he is never tempted to taste disobedience to God. But if you repudiate this knowledge of both, this twofold faculty of discernment, unwittingly you destroy your humanity (IV, 39,1; trans. Saward).

God permitted these things to happen, continues Irenaeus, for our instruction, so that we learn to be prudent in all things. God planned everything ahead of time for our perfection, so that we might one day grow to understand His ways:

How could man ever have known that he was weak and mortal by nature, whereas God was immortal and mighty if he had not had experience of both? To discover his weakness through suffering is not in any sense evil; on the contrary, it is good not to have an erroneous view of one's own nature... The experience of both [good and evil] has produced in man the true knowledge of God and of man, and increased his love for God (V, 3,1; trans. Saward).

If we take this message of Irenaeus quite as he explained it, we see that he is even grateful that Adam and Eve sinned, because thereby we can all learn to not make the same mistake. God, who can make straight lines out of the crooked ones which we give Him, transformed the sin of Adam and Eve into a great educational influence for all of us. This is not Irenaeus literally, but I think he implies the same.

DEATH, MAN'S TESTIMONY OF OBEDIENCE TO GOD

Denis Minns OP, in his book *Irenaeus*, highlights the positive function of death as envisioned by the Saint of Lyons. Adam and Eve, so reasoned Irenaeus, were told that they would receive something of priceless value in the due course of time. Being adolescents, the two couldn't wait for it to happen in due time. They wanted everything, and they wanted it NOW! When the serpent entered the scene at this critical period, it offered them the chance to become like God instantly. They foolishly seized the bait. Their disobedience was childish, and therefore understandable and excusable, but it was grave disobedience nevertheless and carried with it serious consequences (*Proof* 12). It was a refusal to accept the fact that they were creatures, not gods. It was also a refusal to wait for the gift of likeness to God which they would receive only when they would become mature enough to bear it. All of this was implicit in the command given by God that they were not to eat of the fruit of the tree of knowledge of what is good and what is bad (*Ad. Haer.* 4,38,4; Minns p. 62).

It became absolutely necessary, after the sin, that Adam and Eve become obedient to God, and that they demonstrate this submission by action. It was therefore an act of God's mercy toward Adam and Eve that He allowed death to come into their lives. "Death itself was made to serve in the accomplishment of the divine plan, for, by the experience of death, humankind would learn that likeness to God was to be had as a gift from God and at the time appointed by God, and not to be seized by the earth creature as if he had a right to it" (Minns p. 65, on *Ad. Haer.* 4,38,4). Death, then, became the gateway to receive according to God's way the prize which our first parents had tried to seize illegally. The saint thus makes death to be not primarily a punishment of Adam and Eve and their offspring, but rather the gateway through which they must pass in order to receive the longed-for gift of heaven. By dying physically humans can express their subjection and obedience to their Creator. Their over-eager adolescent attitude of rebellion can thus be tamed and overcome by their acceptance of death as a sign of their creaturehood. To die has a great meaning for us, he even enthuses, because death heightens the joy of the resurrection which comes after death:

> This, then, was the great-heartedness of God. He allowed humankind to endure all things and to come to know death so that it might come to the resurrection from the dead. That humankind might

learn by experience what it had been freed from, and be always grateful to the Lord for the gift of incorruptibility received from him (*Adv. Haer.* 3,-20,11-2; trans. of Minns, p. 66).

SANCTIFYING GRACE

Elsewhere Irenaeus speaks of three modes of Adam, "caro, anima, et spiritus" literally "flesh, soul, and spirit." The spirit saves and gives configuration; the flesh provides (bodily) shape and makes us one piece; the soul is between the two, and is capable of taking on either of the two modes: the soul sometimes follows the spirit and is then elevated by it; at other times it consents to the flesh and is then drawn downwards into earthly concupiscence (V,9,1). The flesh, without the Spirit of God, is dead; it has no life; it cannot possess the Kingdom of God (V 9,3).

"Everyone will allow that we are composed of a body taken from the earth, and a soul which receives the spirit from God," he continues (III,22,1). Note that body and soul are natural endowments. For Irenaeus this natural man is not yet a complete and perfect man (cf. Quasten I, 309). To complete man's life, the Spirit of God crowns the soul with His presence and His life. Later theologians would spell out more clearly the doctrine of sanctifying grace (spirit) which elevates the soul to a higher level of being.

It is by recognizing God, states Irenaeus, that a person renews himself. He is renewed "according to the image of the Creator," as he had been made in the beginning. And in the splendor of this renewed form, the person is prepared for the resurrection and for eternal life in heaven.

For the Word of God who made all things, who formed man from the beginning, and who found His creature corrupted by evil, cared for him in every manner: this He did for each and every member because each is of His making; this He did by restoring to man complete health and integrity in preparation for the resurrection. (V,12,5-6).

This is Irenaean theology in combat with the gnostic heresies of his time: Christ restores that eternal life to us which we had once possessed in the first Adam. As he puts it later: "Saving finally in Himself what had been lost at the beginning in Adam" (V,14,1). Christ took flesh precisely so that in the same flesh as Adam had, not in some other, He would recapitulate and seek out that which had been lost (V, 14,2).

GOD CREATES EACH SOUL

Moreover, God endows each human with a personal soul by which he can do good and so merit eternal life, or fail in good and so merit punishment. The soul (anima) of each person is created directly by God, and is not a used second-hand product affected by another in some previous life: "God is not so poor and indigent that he would not give to each body its own soul and character. Consequently when the number (of souls) which He Himself had previously decided upon is completed, all those who are registered as living will arise, having their own bodies and souls and spirits in which they pleased God" (II,33,5).

CONCLUSION

Fr. Stephen J. Duffy, S.J. provides this horizon-spanning

bird's eye view of Irenaeanism: "For Irenaeus, the unification of creation and redemption in a single order is pivotal. Perfection is at the end, not at the beginning; hope burns not for restored innocence but for healing and homecoming. According to Irenaeus, since ethical perfection cannot come ready-made, God made the world a testing ground, and history a person-making process of growth. Adam was no superman tumbling down from perfection to imperfection. Rather he came from his maker's hand childlike... Created imperfect, they were perfectible as they grope through a situation in which sin is virtually inescapable" (Duffy, 619).

For Irenaeus, original sin is not a finalized tragedy, a closed book of the past. It is a lesson by which the Good Shepherd teaches not only Adam and Eve but all of us. "Recapitulation is for Irenaeus a taking up in Christ of all since the beginning. God rehabilitates the earlier divine plan for the salvation of mankind which was interrupted by the fall of Adam, and gathers up the entire work from the beginning to renew, to restore, to reorganize in His incarnate Son who in this way becomes for us a second Adam" (Quasten, I, 295). Christ rehabilitated the original plan of God and did not embark on a new one: "He (the Lord) had himself, therefore, flesh and blood, recapitulating in himself not a certain other, but that original handiwork of the Father, seeking out that which had perished" (5,14,2).

Chapter 14

PRE-AUGUSTINE FATHERS

TERTULLIAN'S TRADUCIANISM

For Tertullian (155-c.220), a professional lawyer from Carthage in Africa, the concepts of Irenaeus about original sin were vague, therefore unsatisfactory. Irenaeus had conceived that Adam, in some <u>mystic sense</u>, included all his descendants in his act of committing original sin. Tertullian sniffed at mystic meanings. This lawyer had a passion for precise expressions, and pioneered much of our theological terminology. He was less fortunate, however, in the invention of the theory of "Traducianism" by which novelty he sought to explain how Adam's descendants shared in Adam's sin by existing in his loins.

He stated (erroneously) that Adam generated not only the <u>bodies</u> of his posterity but also their <u>souls</u>. We were all in Adam when he sinned, so asserted Tertullian, because his soul is the father of all souls of subsequent offspring. Such is the sense of his "<u>ita omnis anima eo usque in Adam censetur donec in Christo recenseatur</u>" (<u>De Anima</u>, 40; see F.R. Tennant 330). "Thus every soul is considered to be in Adam until it is considered anew to be in Christ."

Tertullian, always blunt in his writings and usually highly charged with anger, gave to the Church a treasure of theological terminology by which the Roman Church could define dogmas sharply and avoid pitfalls of ambiguity which dogged the Eastern Church and sometimes tore her apart. For this he deserves praise. But not for his doctrine of Traducianism.

Patience was not Tertullian's strong point. When he wrote about patience he confessed that he felt like an invalid talking about health, himself always sick with the fever of impatience. "Forever a fighter, he knew no relenting towards his enemies, whether pagans, Jews, heretics, or later on, Catholics. All his writings are polemic" (Quasten II,247). He was forever an advocate, out to win his case, to annihilate his adversaries. Eventually he left the Church and joined the Montanists (see Quasten II, 248).

The theory of Traducianism that parents beget the souls of their children as well as their bodies was never accepted by the Church. In a sense the theory would make the souls we receive at conception "second hand" souls, already used by our parents and their parents in turn, back through the generations until Adam. One thinks of inheriting vices and spiritual deficits along family lines, such as lying, cheating and gambling.

The truth is quite otherwise. God creates each human soul directly and immediately, by His own hand. We are all new creatures, sparkling and newly minted by God, not hand-me-downs from past generations. Parents present the gametes with their genetic patterns. When these fuse at fertilization, God, if He so wills, creates a new person. The spiritual substance of the soul animates the building blocks of matter to build a body for itself. The building blocks of matter are themselves interchangeable. But when the soul grabs them and engulfs them into its life force, they form the bricks, so to speak, of our body. The soul then shapes the body by following the blue prints written into the genes. The parents present the bricks as building material, but God creates the soul from nothing as a new creature who will now live for all eternity.

Looking past Tertullian's mistaken notion that the souls of parents generate the souls of their children, we greet him as the original articulator of the Church's basic and durable doctrine that all mankind inherits original sin through descent from Adam. He taught correctly that every person born into this world enters with a sinful condition of soul, being spiritually defiled. His sharp mind perceived this to be a cardinal part of the faith. Based on this belief, the Church baptizes infants, following a tradition which goes back to the time of the apostles.

Tertullian's theory that parents generate the souls as well as the bodies of their children, was a belief held at the time by Stoic philosophers. Applying this mistaken notion to the doctrine of original sin, Tertullian thought the devil had corrupted Adam's soul. Adam, in turn, generated corrupted souls in his descendants. In the words of Tertullian:

> Every soul, then, by reason of its birth, has its nature in Adam until it is born again in Christ; moreover it is unclean all the while that it remains without this regeneration (Baptism); and because unclean, it is actively sinful, and suffuses even the flesh with its own shame (De Anima, 40).

The inference is that the soul of every person born divides off the continuous line of life connected with Adam; this defiled soul in turn contaminates the body which it receives. It was the Devil who corrupted Adam in the first place and all his descendants states Tertullian elsewhere:

> Through Satan, the corrupter of the whole world, man was at the beginning beguiled into breaking the com-

mandment of God; on that account he was given over to death, and he [Adam] thenceforth made the whole race, infected with his seed, transmitters also of his condemnation (De Test. Animae, 3).

This contamination infused into the soul by the devil is a kind of second nature, a corrupted nature living together with the natural soul which retains its goodness, so thought Tertullian:

> There is, then, besides the evil which supervenes on the soul from the intervention of the evil spirit, an antecedent and in a certain sense, natural, evil which arises from its corrupt origin (ex originis vitio). For, as we have said before, the corruption of our nature is another nature (naturae corruptio alia natura est) having a god and father of its own, namely the author of that corruption. Still there is a portion of good in the soul, of that original, divine and genuine good, which is its proper nature. For that which is derived from God is rather obscured than extinguished (De Anima, 41; for the above quotations see Tennant, 234-5).

The "Traducian" scaffolding for the doctrine is rejected by the Church today (see Catechism of the Catholic Church, No.366). Long ago Lactantius had condemned this error as follows:

> A body may be produced from a body, since something is contributed from both; but a soul cannot be produced from souls, because nothing can depart from a slight and incomprehensible subject. Therefore the manner of the production of

souls belongs entirely to God alone...For nothing but what is mortal can be generated from mortals... From this it is evident that souls are not given by parents, but by one and the same God and Father of all, who alone has the law and method of their birth, since He alone produces them (De opif. 19, 1 ff; see Quasten II,408-9).

St. Ambrose (340-397) repudiated Traducianism; so did St. Jerome (c.342-420) who grumped that this error excluded Tertullian from being a "man of the Church." With such clear opposition from the big powers, Traducianism was excluded from gaining a niche in accepted Church doctrine.

Traducianism nevertheless shaded subsequent theology with a view that original sin is a positive evil substance or quality planted into the soul. The theory assumed wrongly that original sin is a taint on the soul, a positive defect, a palpable evil. As will be explained immediately, we should not think of original sin as a blotch on the soul, but as a deficit of grace which ought to be there but is not. Augustine could not make up his mind to clearly reject Traducianism. For him it was useful to explain his concept of the guilt of original sin. He associated its guilt with concupiscence, especially the sexual drive (J. Tixeront, *History of Dogmas*, II, 472). He named the pleasure of sexual intercourse as the "disease of lust" (e.g. *City of God* 14:24).

Even in Thomas the idea lingers that parents, in the act of generation, provide a corrupted mode to the body which then corrupts the soul at the time of animation (Cf. *Summa Theologica*, III,31,5). Sexual intercourse becomes, in this concept, an action whereby parents beget a corrupted child. This concept reflected badly on conjugal intercourse itself. Thomas thought that the sexual drive must be in some manner infected by the corrupt product which it delivers: "Now the corruption of original sin is transmitted by the act of generation... Therefore the powers which concur in this act are chiefly said to be infected" (ST I-II,83,4).

Tertullian's strong language, which pictures the devil as having exceedingly corrupted the human soul and human nature, appears to have spooked the minds of theologians thoroughly, even after they discarded his Traducianism. We are not finished with that turbid concept in theological texts even today. Once a mistaken idea gets into the literature, as we know so well, it tends to perpetuate itself. Subsequent correction in the fine print does not dislodge an entrenched error easily.

The association of sexual intercourse in marriage with the transmission of a positive evil might have been avoided, had original sin been viewed not as a stain on the soul, a positive corruption, but as the absence of a perfection which ought to be there. We recognize it as a <u>deprivation</u> of grace, an absence of the gift of supernatural life which the person ought to have. Parents who beget children cooperate with God in giving them the greatest blessing they can give: life. They do their children a double favor when they quickly remedy their original deprivation of sanctifying grace by promptly bringing them to the baptismal font. There is no excuse today for perpetuating the false concept of Tertullian that sexual intercourse begets a tainted child and that conjugal union in the marital state is therefore somehow associated with evil.

ORIGEN: PRE-EXISTENCE OF SOULS

Origen (185-253) was blessed with a father who educated his eldest son carefully in the Scriptures. This same father gave him the good example, in the year 202, of laying down his life in martyrdom as a witness to the faith. The young Origen was also blessed with a wise and resourceful mother: when her son burned with zeal to run out and join his father in martyrdom, she hid his clothes so that he could not leave the house (Quasten II, 37).

A year later, in 203, Bishop Demetrius put the young Origen in charge of the famous School of Alexandria. He proved to be an intellectual giant, a prodigy with an encyclopedic mind. He also drew to his school capable students who then greatly influenced the intellectual currents of the Church. Fortunately he had a wealthy patron, Ambrose, who helped him to bring into shape and produce a prodigious amount of writings - perhaps 6000 treatises (Epiphanius; see Quasten II, 43). Church historian Eusebius tells how he did it at the urging of a great benefactor, Ambrose:

It was at this period that Origen started work on his *Commentaries on Holy Scripture,* at the urgent request of Ambrose, who not only exerted verbal pressure and every kind of persuasion, but supplied him in abundance with everything needful. Shorthand-writers more than seven in number were available when he dictated, relieving each other regularly, and at least as many copyists, as well as girls trained in penmanship, all of them provided most generously with everything needful at Ambrose's expense (Eusebius, *His. eccl.* 6,23,1-2).

For twenty eight years (203-231) he presided at the School of Alexandria as an intellectual and formative leader in the Church. Unfortunately, influenced by the philosophy of Plato, he theorized that souls are fallen celestial spirits who are re-incarnated. In a former life they offended God. God then punished them by banishing them from the celestial sphere. He cast them down to earth and imprisoned them into human bodies for purification and restoration. Each of us born into this world takes along the baggage of a history of a former sinful life. Each has abused the free will in a previous existence. This, his earlier theory, he developed in his *De Principiis*, I,5,6,7 (see Tennant 297). The sins these souls committed in their previous life limits the amount of grace they receive in the present life:

> Whence some are found from the very commencement of their lives to be of more active intellect, others again of a slower habit of mind, and some are born wholly obtuse, and altogether incapable of instruction (*De Princ.* II,9,3-4).

> Is it not more in conformity with reason, that every soul, for certain mysterious reasons (I speak now according to the opinion of Pythagoras, and Plato, and Empedocles, whom Celsus frequently names), is introduced into a body and is introduced according to its deserts and former actions? (*Contra Cels.* 1,32; see Quasten II,91-92).

In later writings, however, Origen theorized that the entrance of the pre-existing soul into a body which is somehow evil constitutes its original sin (*In Levit.*, VIII,3; *In Lucam,* hom. XIV; P.G., XIII,1834; *Contra Cels.*, VII,50, see J. Tixerant, I, 270). If he implies by this that the bodies were stained by evil because they were descended from Adam who had sinned, he approaches a more satisfactory explanation of original sin, but he did not put the elements together.

Origen modified his views when he moved to Palestinian Caesarea after getting into trouble with Bishop Demetrius in Alexandria. In his new home he came into contact with the practice of infant Baptism. From that time he frequently refers in his writings to a "stain of sin" attached to every human being at birth, needing to be washed away by Baptism. The Jewish ceremony of purification, together with Psalm 51 "in sin my mother conceived me" appears to have influenced his thinking. He gives witness to an Apostolic Tradition about infant Baptism: "For this the Church received a tradition from the Apostles, to baptize even infants" (*Com. in Rom* 5; see Tennant 300).

ATHANASIUS: "ADAM RETURNED TO NATURAL CONDITION"

St. Athanasius (c.297-373), the orthodox hammer of heretics, became the Bishop of Alexandria a century after Origen had left it. His life-long battle was against Arianism. A champion of tradition rather than a pathfinder, he nevertheless developed considerably the doctrine of original sin.

He did not qualify original sin as the cause of a corruption of nature itself, and of our natural faculties. Rather, he saw original sin as the reason why we lapsed back into the natural state, down from an initial higher state which had exceeded our natural constitution (*De Incar.* 4; see Tennant 311). Man was initially created in an extraordinary fashion as an image of the Word in such manner that the knowledge of his own eternity was imprinted on his soul. Man's duty in the initial paradise was to foster and nurture that knowledge by remembering God continually. By so doing he would preserve in himself that image which was the grace and virtue of the Word. He was to lead in paradise a happy and immortal life in familiar consort with His Creator. The soul in this state was pure and free from disturbance by the senses. It could contemplate the Word and in the Word behold the Father Himself. This way of life enraptured man initially and nourished his love (*Contra gentes* 2,8; *Or. de incarn.*, 3; see Tixerant I,137). This concept of a very knowledgeable Adam will be embellished later by Ambrose and Augustine, who will dress him up as a near-celestial being, a superman.

By his sin, continues Athanasius, Adam fell from this initial state and was reduced to what he has naturally. He lost his one-time gifts of integrity and of bodily immortality (*Or. de. incar.* 3,4). In his soul he remained intelligent and immortal, but his knowledge of God dimmed. He also yielded by degrees to sensual pleasures. Jesus Christ can reestablish in man the divine likeness and thus restore to him the knowledge of God (*Contra gentes*, 8).

During the controversy against the Arians St. Athanasius articulated a clear distinction between the act by which God <u>creates</u> us, and the act by which He <u>adopts</u> us as His sons. By creation God gives us our nature, by adoption He establishes us in grace. Our adoption as sons results from the fact that we are the abode of the Word and of the Holy Spirit (*C. Arianos*, II,58,59; III,10; see Tixerant I,138).

After the first sin of Adam, continued Athanasius, those who were born into this already established sinful condition made sinners of themselves in turn. Mankind thus brought evil upon itself through sinning beyond measure. Death began with that first sin, and "corruption thenceforward prevailed against them, gaining even more than its natural power over the whole race" until his misdeeds "passed beyond all measure" (*De Incar.* 5; see Tennant, 312).

CYRIL OF JERUSALEM: "THE WILL REMAINS FREE"

St. Cyril of Jerusalem (315-386), always more of a catechist than a theological innovator, alludes to the results of Adam's sin almost parenthetically without developing the concept. This probably indicates that he holds and teaches what was then commonly accepted among his colleagues in the Eastern Church. Adam's Fall had the universal consequence that all men must die. From this death Christ will rescue us through His Resurrection: "If the first man formed out of the earth brought in universal death, shall not He who formed him out of the earth bring in everlasting life, being Himself life?" (*Cat.* 13,2; see Tennant, 315). Like Irenaeus, Cyril envisions Christ already associating with Adam before the Fall.

The death which Adam's sin brought upon us deprives us of the spiritual life which is from God: "We have been seduced and are lost; is there any chance of salvation? We have fallen... We have been blinded... We have been crippled... In a word, we are dead" (*Cat.* 12,6; see Tennant, 315). Nevertheless he insists that our free will is free indeed and unimpaired, and the devil cannot take this from us (*Cat.* 4,21).

THE TWO GREGORIES OF CAPPADOCIA

St. Gregory of Nazianzus (329-389), whose father was St. Gregory the Elder, whose mother was St. Nonna, was born before his father became the Bishop of Nazianzus. His parents observed celibacy after the father's ordination, in accordance with the tradition. The younger Gregory reared in this family had more talent as an orator than administrator. He is characterized by Tixerant as "a man of a somewhat weak and inconstant character and a thinker of little originality, but the most eloquent of all theologians, who knows how to explain luminously, for the benefit of the weakest intelligences, the loftiest mysteries of faith" (II,7). The Greek language flowed from his pen and tongue with a classic beauty, power, elegance, and eloquence, which none of the Fathers have rivalled. He became known as the "Christian Demosthenes."

This Gregory stated trenchantly that "Adam closed heaven, as he had closed (the garden of) paradise, to all his descendants" (*In Psalm* 118,4,2). The sin of Adam is also "our sin" and is therefore in us (*Orat.* 19,3; see Tennant, 318). But we are not at all totally depraved, and our wills remain free. Christ, though an offspring of Adam, was not begotten by a human father, and therefore by-passed the route by which offspring inherit original sin from their parents.

Gregory of Nyssa (c.330-c.395), "was neither an outstanding administrator and monastic legislator like Basil, nor an attractive preacher and poet like Gregory of Nazianzus. But as a speculative theologian and mystic he is certainly the most gifted of the three great Cappadocians" (Quasten, *Patrology III*, 254). Brushing aside the claim of

Origen that human souls pre-existed in another world before they were imprisoned into human bodies on this earth, he had Adam and Eve begin their existence on this earth. But he then made the paradise of Adam and Eve into an exotic world, essentially different from the one we know. Origen had claimed that members of our present human race had previously tasted a heaven-like life in another and higher world. Gregory doesn't avert to a former life, but holds that paradise itself was a place and condition where our first parents once lived almost like the angels.

The sin of our first parents brought death into the world, made man to be mortal, and subjected him to the downward pull of concupiscence, said Gregory of Nyssa, a forerunner now to Augustine. Our whole nature was weakened, he added for good measure, and our understanding was darkened when sin entered this angelic paradise (*De orat. domin*. 4; see Tennant, 323). Had our first parents not sinned, they would have lived much as the angels, not marrying nor being married, nor generating offspring. They would have multiplied after the manner of the angels (De Hom. Opif. cc.16,17; Tennant 320). (This supposition was never adopted by the Church.)

To partake of Adam's nature by descent is to participate also in his post-sin condition, and in his Fall. This inborn sin is removed by Baptism (*Orat. Cat*. c. 35; Tennant, 322). Gregory thereby asserts that death which is now natural to us, and concupiscence, and a hereditary moral taint on the soul, are consequences of original sin. We inherit all this from Adam. The stage is now set for further elaboration of these concepts by the great mind of St. Augustine.

Chapter 15

THE GENIUS OF SAINT AUGUSTINE

PELAGIUS NEGATES ORIGINAL SIN

When a British monk by the name of Pelagius and his companion Celestius fled from Rome to Africa in 410, before the hordes of Aleric who sacked the city, the battle between Augustine and Pelagius was engaged. The Bishop of Hippo, who in future would be called the Doctor of Grace, was not amused by what he heard. Julian, Bishop of Eclanum in Italy, well known to Augustine, had given systematic form to the innovations of the Pelagian group. Essentially, it was a form of "Do-It-Yourself-Christianity" dispensing with the need of the Redeemer, Christ. "Use your native will power, control yourself, save yourself," is his jingoistic way of salvation when stripped of ornament.

Pelagius, a spiritual director of eager ascetic believers, moved from England to Rome during the 390's. He had all the appearances, and muttered all the pious words, of a holy man. He was given to ascetic practices and soon gained acceptance and admiration in this leading city, especially among the elite and pious. He soon acquired powerful friends and alliances also in southern Italy, in France at Arles, and in Jerusalem.

He considered the contemporary teachings on original sin to be a hindrance rather than a help in the battle to acquire holiness of life. He regarded the doctrine to be a soporific comfort to assuage spiritual slothfulness. Believers should cultivate their spiritual lives by vigorous self-improvement exercises, he urged. "You can do it!" he preached. The sin of Adam is not at all transmitted to descendants by some kind of inheritance. It does not inhibit our spiritual vigor. Descendants do indeed imitate Adam's sin, but they do not inherit what was his personal act. Soon he was saying that death and concupiscence are natural to humans, not a punishment for Adam's sin. Then he went overboard advising that the Baptism of children is not needed for a remission of sin because they had neither committed sins, nor had they inherited original sin. He conceded, however, that it might wisely be administered as a sign of acceptance by the Church. It also enables them to reach the Kingdom of Heaven, which, so he claimed, is a higher state of blessedness than eternal life.

Zealous to arouse the Christians in Rome from a state of spiritual listlessness, Pelagius stressed the power of human freedom and the role of man's own moral effort to achieve salvation. External rules and good example, he asserted, can help us to achieve salvation. His teachings implied that there is no absolute need for the gift of God's grace as an internal help to capacitate the mind and will for supernatural works. The system he championed, which was influenced by Stoic Philosophy, claimed that man alone can achieve salvation by his natural powers. Pelagius regarded grace as a natural ability of man. He thus attempted to construct a closed system of man saving himself, without absolute need of assistance of supernatural divine help. The system is not far from current advocates of a "do-it-yourself" religion.

Pelagius made a pious show of being shocked and scandalized by Augustine's teaching that a man cannot remain chaste by his own effort and determination, without the help of God's grace. If that be the case, he asserted, then man is not free. He insisted that man has a natural capacity to live a sinless and holy life and so to merit eternal bliss by virtue of his own natural powers. The teachings of the Scriptures, the law, and the example of Christ, are additional booster helps toward salvation but they are not essential. Grace, he taught, facilitates an understanding of God's commandments, and is a help toward obeying them. But he subtly denied that man really needs grace absolutely to capacitate the will to obey the commandments. Humans can turn away from sin and perform Christian works of merit by their natural innate powers, he said in effect. That's where Augustine, the Doctor of Grace, picked up the scent.

The teachings of Pelagius, however, were cast into pious form and filled with ambiguities. It required a genius like St. Augustine to see through the subterfuges. His keen mind detected that Pelagius denies the absolute need of grace to achieve salvation. There is no need in such a system for Christ our Savior, who forgives our sins, who assists us internally to lead a life of faith and holiness. In a treatise written in 418 Augustine cuts through the subtle ambiguity of Pelagian errors and exposes the system's lack of humility and faith. He wrote, for example:

> In like manner, in another passage of the same book he (Pelagius) says: "In order that men may more easily accomplish by grace that which they are commanded to do by free will." ... The addition of the words "more easily," ... tacitly suggests the possibility of accomplishing good works even without the grace of God. But such a meaning is disallowed by Him who says, "Without me ye can do nothing." (John 15,5; Chap.30 of *On the Grace*

of Christ, see <u>Basic</u> <u>Writings</u> I,604).

The system is basically naturalistic, and excludes as superfluous traditional teachings about original sin and Redemption. The sacraments thus become ornamental rituals, not channels of grace coming from Christ. Their administration becomes impious hypocrisy. Redemption by Christ is essentially denied (see explanation, e.g. in Quasten, *Patrology IV*, 479-81). Pelagius preached strict demands of an austere life, urging people to get hold of themselves by self control and sheer will power. But when subterfuges are removed, he did not make humans dependent on Christ's internal help to achieve salvation. An intimate and loving dependence on Christ is not in his system.

> Any inter-relation of love, confidence, gratitude disappears. Prayer is a non-sense. The theory was, in fact, a most radical deformation of the very essence of Christianity, and it must produce inevitably in all who hold it a corresponding deformity of character. The Pelagians, for whom humility was an impossibility, were, in their spiritual life, really cultivating themselves. Their own spiritual achievement was the chief object of their attention, and with their theory all the harsh pride of the Stoics returned to the Christian Church (Philip Hughes, *A History of the Church, II*,15-16).

AUGUSTINE ENGAGES PELAGIUS

Pelagius and Celestius came to Africa in 410, the former stopping only briefly on his way to Jerusalem. But Celestius made no secret of the new doctrine, and asked to be admitted to the presbyterate of Carthage. Augustine regarded their teachings as "a new scandal in the Church" (*Ep.* 177,15), "a new heresy" (*Retract.* 2,33; see Quasten, *Patrology IV,* 464). In 411 the clergy and Bishop of Carthage condemned six elements found in the teachings of Pelagianism which they claimed to be heretical.

Though condemned in Africa, Pelagius gained an important friend in John, Bishop of Jerusalem. Smooth talk, ambiguous language, and politics gave him breathing space. But Jerome at nearby Bethlehem opposed him in 414. Pelagian ruffians rewarded Jerome for this by burning down his monasteries (*Patrology IV,* 218). Pelagius was acquitted at the Council of Diospolis in December 415, and then explained his thought systematically in the book *De Libero Arbitrio*. He wrote a letter to Pope St. Innocent I, claiming that the process against himself and his doctrine were calumny. Pope St. Zosimus, successor of Innocent, was deceived for a time by this letter. He wrote to Africa in November 417 that Pelagius was the victim of the malice of the bishops.

But Augustine, who had read the heretical works carefully, remained convinced that the assessment of Pope Zosimus must be wrong. If Pelagius is right, then grace is not a supernatural help from God. It is really only free human effort (Augustine, *De Gestis* 10,22; *Patrology IV*, 479). The African Bishops sent an elaborate reply to Pope Zosimus on March 21, 418. This enabled the Pope to distinguish the real Pelagius from the disguise of his false front. It was now his turn to act decisively. Pope Zosimus sent an approving reply to the African Bishops. They then opened what would become the famous Council of Carthage which condemned Pelagianism. St. Augustine played a decisive role in this 16th Council of Carthage which, like a continental divide, delineates compellingly doctrines on grace and original sin.

THE END OF THE PELAGIAN HERESY

Upon receiving the canons formulated at Carthage, Pope St. Zosimus issued the *Tractoria*. In it he approved some of the canons, but apparently not the one on immunity from bodily death in paradise. He also asked the local bishops to sign a prescribed form of condemnation. Eighteen Bishops of southern Italy had no trouble with the condemnation of the teachings of Pelagius as such, but they were reluctant to indicate their agreement with Augustine's theories. They repudiated what they styled "the African Dogma," and the Pope promptly deposed them. Its leader, Julian, Bishop of Eclanum, eventually moved in with Theodore of Mopsuestia, and was never reinstated in Eclanum.

The heresy survived in England until Bishop Germanus of Auxerre, sent by the Pope, made orthodoxy to prevail there in 447. Thus the Pelagian heresy was condemned as incompatible with the faith and came to an end as an organized religion (see Hughes II,18). The towering figure of Augustine played an essential role in its organizational demise.

MAGISTERIAL TEACHINGS ON ORIGINAL SIN

After St. Augustine died in 430 a catalogue of approved doctrine about original sin, grace, and freedom was drawn up, which gradually acquired great authority due mainly to tacit approval by the universal Church. This so-called "*Indiculus*" lists what "the most holy see of the blessed apostle Peter has sanctioned and taught" concerning heresy, the grace of God and free will." The list skips Canon 1 - 2 of Carthage (physical death) but includes canons 3 - 5 as having been promulgated by Pope Zosimus in the *Tractoria* of 418. For the Catholics of the next thousand years it teaches about the powers, the need, and the blessed value of grace, and the need of prayer to obtain this gift. The heart of the teaching is contained in Chapter One as follows:

> Chap. 1: In Adam's sin all men lost their natural power for good and their innocence. No one can of his own free will rise out of the depth of this fall if he is not lifted up by the grace of the merciful God. This is the pronouncement of Pope Innocent of blessed memory in his letter to the Council of Carthage: "He (Adam) acted of his own free will when he used his gifts thoughtlessly; he fell into the abyss of sin; he sank, and he found no means to rise again. Betrayed by his freedom for ever, he would have remained weighed down by his fall had not later the advent of Christ raised him by His grace when through the cleansing of a new regeneration he washed away all previous guilt in the bath of His Baptism." (DS 239; Dupuis 503)...

By the help of grace, continued the *Indiculus*, free will is not destroyed but liberated and supported. "For such is God's goodness towards all men that He wants His own gifts to be our merits and that He will give us an eternal reward for what He has bestowed upon us" (DS 248; Dupuis 1914). This beautiful doctrine, then, became the common heritage of the Church.

As noted elsewhere, however, Trent did not incorporate

Canon One of the Council of Carthage (418), so dear to the heart of Augustine. It reads as follows:

> 1) This has been decided by all the bishops...gathered together in the holy Synod of Carthage: Whoever says that Adam, the first man, was made mortal in the sense that he was to die a bodily death whether he sinned or not, which means to quit the body would not be a punishment for sin but a necessity of nature, <u>anathema</u> <u>sit</u> (DS 222; Dupuis 501).

Augustine, the soul of Carthage, was convinced that original sin was the cause of physical death in Adam: "And therefore it is agreed among all Christians who truly hold the Catholic faith that we are subject to the death of the body, not by the law of nature, by which God ordained no death for man, but by His righteous infliction on account of sin; for God, taking vengeance on sin, said to the man, in whom we all then were, 'Dust thou art and unto dust thou shalt return'" (*City of God* 13:15). Augustine was certain about this, but others were apparently not so sure.

Pope St. Zosimus may indeed have refused to promulgate this Canon One, which the *Indiculus* also omitted, and which Trent would by-pass eleven hundred years later. The apparent omission of this Canon in the *Tractoria* promulgated by Pope Zosimus in 418, in which other canons of Carthage 418 were promulgated, may have hurt St. Augustine, who thereafter failed to capitalize on this singular item. He would likely have made much of it had the Pope seen fit to promulgate it. The Fathers of Trent, in 1546, initially drafted a sentence stating that Adam would not have died physically had he not sinned. Later, however, at the request of many of the Fathers the sentence was deleted and Trent did not finally define such a teaching.

THE INFLUENCE OF SAINT AUGUSTINE

When Saint Augustine battled against the Pelagians, writes Hughes:

> The need of the moment brought from him the work which is his chief title to glory as a theologian, the construction of a whole theory to explain the original state of man, the nature and effect of the first man's fall, the nature of the Redemption, and the way in which, in virtue of the Redemption, God acts upon the souls of the redeemed. It is a work in which he had singularly little help from preceding writers, and a work which was to give rise, as it still gives rise, to passionate discussions; a work, too, since proved erroneous in more than one point, but a work which in its main lines has long since passed into the traditional theology of the Catholic Church (Hughes II,18).

Perhaps the heat of the battle against Pelagius influenced Augustine to exaggerate the beatitude of Adam before the Fall, and to counter-exaggerate human misery after it. The saint saw in the earlier Adam an extraordinary harmonious union of reason and senses, an intellect infused by God with immense knowledge, and a body which might escape physical death if he persevered in grace. When he sinned he lost these extraordinary gifts together with sanctifying grace. The Fall of Adam, he laments initiated the chronic misery of mankind from which no man escapes, the opposition between spirit and flesh. Here he views man's present condition more pessimistically than does St. Irenaeus.

The strong appetite in man for sexual pleasure, together with its lack of simple obedience to control by the will, influenced Augustine to believe that the drive is disordered by reason of original sin. He did not perceive human nature to be radically vitiated because of the sin, but he did attribute to it a resultant inherited weakness, a discounted version of our natural faculties that is now transmitted to all who possess a human nature. He was convinced that all mankind lost not only sanctifying grace through original sin, but also special gifts of integrity which he attributed to Adam before his sin.

Augustine's doctrines on grace and the Mystical Body of Christ, the above gloomy perceptions notwithstanding, are a priceless heritage of the Church for all times. In the new arrangement under Christ, he recognizes, it is God who provides even the first help to believe. Humanity is being re-created by incorporation into Christ, made one with Him in Baptism, nourished by Him in the Eucharist. Believers are not isolated individuals in separate unions with Christ, but are one corporate union in Him: "This idea of the salvation of Humanity as the members of Christ -- members of a body whose head is the God-Man -- is the very heart of St. Augustine's theology" (Hughes, 19). Grace is the circulatory system of this body. This luminous teaching is the very antithesis of the do-it-yourself religion of Pelagius.

It is really Jesus Christ who prays, who lives, who performs the saving acts of the individual believer, taught Augustine. It is St. Paul re-thought, the tradition set out afresh with new profundity, new lucidity, with passionate fervor, disciplined logic and a wholly new rhetorical splendor, in answer to the menace of Pelagius's sterilizing divorce of man from God in the spiritual life (cf. Hughes, 20).

But the system which St. Augustine constructed is not without difficulties, continues Hughes, particularly in the matter of adjusting the relations between God's activity through grace and man's free will. These difficulties remain in part even today, when theologians dispute as keenly about them as they did in the time of St. Augustine.

Beside the doctrine on grace, Augustine's vast writings are a bridge of culture across the centuries, a treasure of humanity.

> He was almost the whole intellectual patrimony of medieval Catholicism, a mine of thought and erudition which the earlier Middle Ages, for all its delving, never came near to exhausting. He was the bridge between two worlds, and over that bridge there came to the Catholic Middle Ages something of the educational ideals and system of Hellenism; there came the invaluable cult of the ancient literature, the tradition of its philosophy and all the riches of Christian Antiquity.

> In St. Augustine were baptized, on that momentous Easter Day of 387, the schooling, the learning, the learned employments, and the centuries of human experience in the ways of thought, which were to influence and shape all the medieval centuries...From his masterly understanding there comes the most masterly presentation hitherto seen, and which will endure for nearly a thousand years

without a rival, until there comes another mind, as great as his own, and equipped with still better instruments (Hughes, 20-21).

We close with a sample of the saint's doctrine about grace and the free will, a lesson surely needed in our day no less than in his, because the struggle to control the sex instinct and integrate it into human growth and maturity is never easy. His trust in grace is absolute, based no doubt on the experience of grace in his own life: "God does not command the impossible, but in commanding He admonishes you to do that which you can and to ask for that which you cannot" (*On Nature and Grace*, 50). So speaks Augustine, who, with the help of grace, pulled himself free from the strangling grip of the habit of sins against chastity, who then founded a monastic way of life to help the clergy devote themselves to God and fellowmen in full measure by a complete gift of self in celibate love.

The immense power of Augustine for good in the Church remains, but it cannot be denied that, when fencing with Pelagius to uphold the necessity of grace for salvation, he adopted a pessimistic view of man's natural endowments. He also asserted that Adam's sin initiated concupiscence in our human lives, and that it made humans physically mortal on this earth. The Fathers of the Council of Trent, eleven hundred years later, hesitated to affirm that these two points belong to the deposit of the faith.

Chapter 16

CHRIST, PANTOKRATOR

Christ is the Alpha and Omega whose greatness we celebrate at the Easter Vigil before lighting the candles. The priest intones these memorable words while tracing the symbols of the resurrection into the new Easter Candle:

> Christ yesterday and today
> the beginning and the end
> Alpha and Omega
> all time belongs to him
> and all the ages
> to him be glory and power
> through every age for ever. Amen.

If all time and all the ages belong to Christ, then it would appear to be appropriate that God ought to consult with Christ -- with His human mind and heart also -- while creating and arranging the history of all times and ages. The sentence proclaimed by Pope John Paul II comes to mind: "In Jesus Christ the Father created the world" (To Special Synod Assembly of Asia, 14 May 1998). Christ was not yet Incarnate according to the manner by which we measure time as "before and after;" but in eternity the sequences of our "before and after" are absorbed into ageless duration. Christ could already be present to God and in operation in eternity, before He meshed Himself into the churning cogs of time on earth.

The cosmos must be Christ's at all times; it is His inheritance; He is its General Manager -- its CEO. Paul saw that God already chose us in Christ from eternity: "Who has blessed us in Christ with every spiritual blessing in the heavenly places even as he chose us in him before the foundation of the world" (Eph 1:3). God already prepared our good works for us in Christ from eternity: "For we are his workmanship, created in Christ Jesus for good works, which God prepared beforehand, that we should walk in them" (Eph 2:10). God had Christ at His right hand when, from eternity, He pulled the lever to detonate the cosmos into being. The Book of Proverbs savors the event with lovely poetry:

> When he established the heavens I was there,
> when he drew a circle on the face of the deep,
> when he made firm the skies above,
> when he established the fountains of the deep,
> when he assigned to the sea its limit,
> so that the waters might not transgress his command,
> when he marked out the foundations of the earth,
> then I was there beside him, like a master workman;
> and I was daily his delight,
> rejoicing before him always,
> rejoicing in his inhabited world,
> and delighting in the sons of men (Prov 8:27-31).

If Christ, foreseen on the platform of eternity before time began, is pictured by God to be delighted with the cosmos and with the sons of men, then each of us already existed in Him in anticipation of our birth; and in anticipation of His birth in Bethlehem. It is then not unrealistic to contemplate that God created all things with Christ always in mind; with Christ always at His side as prime Consultant. The cosmos is to be truly Christ-dominated, His habitat of choice.

He would want to experience the delights of family life in a warm domestic circle in Nazareth, where His foster father Joseph would cherish His mother Mary with a pure love fortified by perfect chastity; where Joseph would model for Him the image of human manhood, point out to him the lilies of the field and the birds of the air, forecast the weather by evening red and morning gray, guide His hand firmly upon the tools of carpentry, do business sagaciously with all manner of customers coming to the shop, take interest in community life and speak up when necessary, stand up to read in the Synagogue when called upon.

Nazareth should be a home with a resourceful mother who knew well how to manage the house, its kitchen, laundry and playroom; who taught Him to speak correctly and in a pleasant manner; who modelled for Him graciousness of etiquette and correct manners with people; who traced with Him the constellations of the stars in the vault of the sky at night; a strong woman who was an implacable enemy of all evil, even the shadow of it; who imaged for Him true love for all people; whose heart was one with His in love for the Father, in love for all men even unto the end. She grew together with Him into the compassionate Woman who would stand by during His agony on the cross; who would bow her head when He breathed His last and died. All this and more.

Christ, we say, ought rightfully be recognized as the architect and planner of our cosmos, which He Himself filled with beauty and adventure, with love and splendor, with passion and pathos, with victories and human triumphs; there are also partial and temporary victories obtained by the Devil and by evil persons which inevitably turn out to be their own undoing. May the marvelous cosmos, so

carefully designed by Christ, serve mankind well for ages
yet to come! May the end of this beautiful world be millennia beyond our day!

THE IMMENSE KNOWLEDGE OF CHRIST

A woman's bleeding had baffled her doctors. For twelve
years her hemorrhages had not been cured, although she
had spent all her livelihood on medical experts. Then she
touched the tassel of the cloak of Jesus, and "immediately
her bleeding stopped" (Lk 8:44). Whatever medical problem was involved, Jesus knew all about it -- and cured by
the power of His will the abnormality which His mind had
identified.

The storm at sea frightened even the seasoned fishermen
as their boat began to ship water. Fearful of sinking into
the waves they awakened Jesus. "And he awoke and
rebuked the wind and the raging waves; and they ceased,
and there was a calm" (Lk 8:24). In His mind the Godman
had measured the energy of the storm and the inertia of
the lapping waves. With His will He ironed the waves
smooth and blocked the wind from its blowing. He took
care to prevent a destructive vacuum from developing
downwind after He had suddenly stopped the flow of air
from upwind. The cosmos was safe in the hands of its
Master Designer.

Lazarus was dead four days now. Martha blurted out that
there would be a stench. Jesus knew well that raising the
corpse from the dead would be no small feat. Thirteen
billion nerves of the brain would need to be reactivated,
over seventy trillion cells should be re-conditioned. A
stiffened heart would have to resume rhythmic beating. No

problem! "Lazarus, come out!" spoke Jesus. "The dead man came out, his hands and feet bound with bandages, his face wrapped with a cloth. Jesus said to them 'Unbind him, and let him go'" (Jn 11:43-44). Lazarus stood there re-conditioned, good as new.

The architect of the cosmos already knew everything there was to be known about the compaction of this created material -- having Himself designed and created it by His divine power, and having witnessed the designing of it with His created human intelligence. He knew well the bricks and mortar of its constitutive elements -- the particles, atoms, molecules -- for even now His divine power was preserving it in being. Every cell of the human body He knew, each a workshop enclosed by a membrane of double walls fitted with ionic gateways and pumps, structured with microtubules, governed by RNA and DNA directing its reactions with lightning speed, each cell coordinated with the entire throbbing body by way of the diversified network of the 100,000 genes of the human genome. The Godman was not a stranger in the cosmos. He knew and governed its micro-particles and balanced in His hands the 100 billion galaxies moving outward from the center of the cosmos to expand the bubble of space.

CHRIST, LIGHT OF THE COSMOS

An ancient Rabbi told this story to explain how God had made the decision to create our world despite the sinfulness which He foresaw:

Yahweh said, "How can I create the world, when these godless people will rise up and revolt against me?" But when God saw Abraham who was to come, he said, "Look, I have found a rock on which I can construct and establish the world." For this reason he called Abraham a rock: "Look at the rock from which you were hewn" (Is 51:1-2).

By his faith, Abraham, the father of all believers, is the rock which supports creation, pushing back Chaos, the original flood which imminently threatens to ruin everything. So spoke the Rabbi. (Told by Cardinal Ratzinger, *Oss. Rom.* 8 July, 1991).

The Rabbi pictured Abraham as the rock against which the filthy tide of rebellion against God would be contained. We know that Abraham was but a foreshadowing of Christ. Against Christ the tide of the world's rebellion would not prevail. This Savior made it His mission to absorb the worst evils that the world and the flesh and the Devil could throw up against Him. He absorbed them, did not take revenge on His enemies, but neutralized all the poisons of evil in His body and spirit by laying down His life as the price of peace of mankind with God. "For our sake he opened his arms on the cross; he put an end to death and revealed the resurrection" (Eucharistic Prayer II).

The Son, when planning the universe with the Father and the Spirit, foresaw the ocean of rebellion which free people would wash against their Creator. But He persevered in His plan, gave the nod to the plan of creation, and resolved to take the punishment for the evil we do into His future body, no matter how painful that would be.

When His hour drew near, Peter attempted to defend Him against the invasion of evil, but Christ would have none of that: "Put your sword into its sheath; shall I not drink the cup which the Father has given me?" (John 18:11). He would allow His beard to be plucked, his face to be slapped, His claims to be called blasphemy. He allowed the nails to fasten Him until they achieved His death, the cross to crucify Him until all the bitterness of sin was drained.

The sin of Adam and His descendants, and the Devil to whom the sin yielded power, would make Christ's life on earth more difficult in the end, as He absorbed the waves and shocks of evil, and gave no rebound. In the end sin died with Him, and He thus put an end to death and readied Himself and His followers for the resurrection. We gaze reflectively upon the scene of the crucifixion, weeping with Jeremiah who lamented what the powers of evil were doing to Jerusalem, figure of Christ:

> The maidens of Jerusalem
>   bow their heads to the ground.
> Worn out from weeping are my eyes,
>   within me all is in ferment;
> My gall is poured out on the ground
>   because of the downfall
>   of the daughter of my people...
> To what can I liken or compare you,
>   O daughter of Jerusalem?...
> For great as the sea is your downfall;
>   who can heal you? (Lam 2 passim).

The resurrection heals totally the destruction done to Christ by the forces of evil. A bolt of lightning announced the Easter Event as an earthquake shook away the stone from the tomb. Evil and the Devil had vainly attempted to liquidate goodness. The risen Christ obliterates negatives from His Church which rises with Him in victory. Only those who choose to make themselves "sons of perdition" (cf. Jn 17:12) and close themselves off terminally from the saving powers of the Son of Man lose their battle against evil.

CHRIST, HIGH PRIEST OF THE COSMOS

In the High Priestly Prayer, Jesus asked the Father to first of all bless His circle of close friends, those at table with Him who were now priests: "Sanctify them in truth... For their sake I consecrate myself, that they also may be consecrated in truth" (John 17:17;19). By consecrating them with Himself, He separated them from secular purposes for an exclusively sacred function. He took for Himself personally the members of the ministerial priesthood. It is this priesthood which is the heart of the mission of Christ's coming into this world.

"Doctor Subtilis" Duns Scotus deems that the Son of God became Incarnate to become the priest of the cosmos, to give glory to God from the platform which God would fashion outside of His eternal dwelling. The Son would become man to reflect glory back to the Godhead from the outside, from out of a created world. As Scotus wrote: God wished to be loved from the outside, by One who can love God with maximal love:

> God first loves Himself; secondly, He loves Himself for others, and this is an ordered love; thirdly, He wishes to be loved by the One who can love Him in the highest way -- speaking of the love of someone who is extrinsic to Him; and fourthly, He foresees the union of that nature which must love Him with the greatest love even if no one had fallen

[into sin] (*Opus Par*.d.7, q.4; see translation, Carol, p. 35).

If I may interpret: God loves Himself and wishes others to share in this bliss. How can He bring this about with maximum amplitude? By having the Son become man, who as God-man can love God as none other can possibly do. And so God decreed the Incarnation, without immediate reference to any original sin at all. Such is the reasoning of Scotus.

Whether the insight of Scotus is correct, or whether Thomas interprets God's mind more correctly by saying that Christ became man in response to the sin of Adam, at any rate, Christ is NOW the Primate of our cosmos. He is commissioned by God to take charge of the universe for the duration, until time comes to an end: "Then comes the end, when he delivers the kingdom to God the Father" (1 Cor 15:24). Before that end comes He recapitulates the human family first of all, and the entire material cosmos as well, into His power and love so long as the clock of time continues to tick its way toward the arrival of the eschaton.

Theologian Matthias Scheeben points out that Christ, by means of His latreutic sacrifice, obtained from God not only the remission of the sins for the human race; He also purchased for us in a positive manner the gift of supernatural grace in the first place:

> Christ has not only regained for us the grace of the children of God, which we had forfeited by sin, in the sense that He has wiped out the sin and thereby enabled the original grace of God to return to its

rightful place; for in that case grace would ever remain pure grace, and would not have been positively purchased by Him. No; just as by the satisfactory efficacy of His sacrifice, He has absolved us of the infinite debt which we had incurred with God, so by the meritorious power of His sacrifice He has made God our debtor; that is, He paid Him so high a price that God no longer bestows upon us that great benefit, the grace of divine sonship, out of sheer, gratuitous kindness and free love, but now confers it upon us as our due. It is here above all that we gain some insight into the meaning, so sublime and mysterious, which the sacrifice of Christ has for us (*The Mysteries of Christianity*, 452-453).

Christ continues on earth, through the Sacrifice of the Mass, the immolation and glorification of His own body, thereby enabling us to likewise consecrate ourselves to God with Him. Scheeben rightly points out that the meaning of death is thus transformed from association with punishment to become instead an act of adoration:

By their union with Him the bodies of His members attain to a higher, mystical consecration. Furthermore, they receive thereby a freedom from death in virtue of which they undergo death not so much as a natural necessity or punishment, but rather, after the example of their head, take death upon themselves for the honor of God. By their immolation, mortifications, and toils of this life and crowned in death, by the immolation which takes place in Christ's members in the spirit and power of Christ, the members are made ready as a fragrant holocaust to enter with Christ into the presence of God in their glorified bodies, and to be received by God. After the general resurrection the whole Christ, head and body, will be a perfect holocaust offered to God for all eternity, since Christ Himself, not only in His personal being, body and soul, but also in His entire mystical body, will be truly universal, total holocaust offered to God through the transforming fire of the Holy Spirit (439).

We laudably believe that by the power of His passion, death, resurrection, and ascension, Christ wins for Himself not only stewardship over the material cosmos, not only Headship of the human race, but universal dominion and power and glory over all the angelic creatures in heaven as well. For the angels, too, Christ offered His sacrifice, "not indeed that it reconciles them to God after sin, but in the sense that the Lamb which was slaughtered in the begin-ning stands eternally in God's sight to merit and secure supernatural grace for them also," so reasons Scheeben (444). He is truly a *Spiritus vivificans*, a life-giving spirit who fills angels as well as humans with divine spirit and life.

Seen in this light, suffering and death are not a minus in our lives; when we accept them fortified with the power of Christ, they open up for us new dimensions of a glorified purpose of life on earth. Without death the meaning of our lives would be comparatively shallow and limited. Had Adam been transformed into a spirit without having under-gone physical death, his sojourn on earth would not have had the richness of meaning which ours has, now that we can grasp death as a supreme act of adoration to God, fortified by the power of Christ. By suffering and dying in obedience to God we activate a supreme love within ourselves which would not be realized in the absence of pain and death. "Suffering thus undertaken is obviously an act of the purest self-sacrifice and the most sublime virtue, and hence is more honorable and lovable than impassibility" (Scheeben, 425).

By His death, resurrection and ascension He is the fire of sacrifice by which the fragrance of the universe rises up to God in adoration and thanksgiving. Through this dedication of the spiritual and material universe in Himself Christ makes the cosmos become one piece, dedicated now to God and to the humming His praises. Without Christ this world would have been a self-enclosed insular secularism, an orchestra of sounding brass and tinkling symbol with no conductor to coordinate the players, no audience to appreciate its significance and beauty.

The cosmos has been created, in this concept, not for its own sake, but to give glory to God. And Christ is the priest who takes this cosmos into Himself as His own, and makes the entire universe sing its obedience to God to give Him glory.

The ministerial priest, who is called to Christ's side to be His alternate, participates in Christ's priestly function as one specially called for this purpose. Like Christ, he is consecrated -- set aside from secular purposes -- to live the cosmic consecration to God. The priest is Christ on earth, consecrating it until He comes again in glory. Until the end of time, the priest, in persona Christi will profess belief in God from the midst of the universe, as Psalm 22 testifies:

> I will tell of thy name to my brethren;
> in the midst of the congregation

I will praise thee...
All the ends of the earth shall remember
and turn to the Lord;
and all the families of the nations
shall worship before him.

Not only the ministerial priest, but all believers in God are called to be a "kingdom of priests" (Ex 19:6) who make this world to be an offering pleasing to God. Those whom Christ marks with the seal of the baptismal priesthood, those whom He inspires to know God, to love Him, to serve Him -- all are elevated by Christ to be priests of the cosmos, who offer glory to God from the midst of the secular universe.

To gather up the cosmos and dedicate it to God, that, in the mind of Scotus, was Christ's primary mission. After Adam sinned, he did not get stuck in that sin but began the struggle to do good with the help of Christ. When Adam's descendants sank into the morass of "the sin of the world," Christ blazed a trail of goodness for all to follow, in ancient times and today. At the end of time, Christ will come again, highly visible, to sort the good from the bad, the sheep from the goats.

CHRIST, DEFINITIVE JUDGE

Michelangelo painted the face of Christ at the Last Judgment not as One instilling fear into the damned, but as One concerned that justice be done to one and all. The face of Christ dominating the wall of the Sistine Chapel makes justice to prevail universally. Mary, at His right, appears to reflect pity and sorrow for those who will not make it to heaven. Ascanio Condivi, an early biographer of Michelangelo, writes about the meaning the artist expressed in this painting:

> Above the angels of the trumpets is the Son of God in majesty, in the form of a man, with arm and strong right hand uplifted. He wrathfully curses the wicked, and drives them from before His face into eternal fire. With His left hand stretched out to those on the right, He seems to draw the good gently to Himself...(Quoted in *Inside the Vatican,* May 1994, p. 28).

We know the reality which will follow this opening scene of the Last Judgment. For Christ has foretold what is to come:

> When the Son of Man comes in his glory, and all the angels with him, he will sit on his glorious throne. Before him will be gathered all the nations, and he will separate them one from another as a shepherd separates the sheep from the goats, and he will place the sheep at his right hand, but the goats at the left. Then the King will say to those at his right hand, "Come, O blessed of my Father, inherit the kingdom prepared for you from the foundation of the world..." Then he will say to those at his left hand, "Depart from me, you cursed, into the eternal fire prepared for the Devil and his angels..." (Mt 25:31-34;41).

ALPHA AND OMEGA

The cosmos began with Christ's consent. "I am the light of the world" (Jn 8:12) He revealed to the unbelieving Pharisees, who become so confused that they thought they had a duty to stone Him to death. They should have bowed their heads to ponder His meaning. He spoke what He knew to be true. For our cosmos became a visible reality when on the first day of creation God said: "Let there be light" and there was light (Gen 1:3). Christ is that light of the cosmos.

Without light, the cosmos would be a jumble of meaning-less chaotic emptiness. It would have no purpose. God would not create a meaningless cosmos. But when God decreed the Incarnation, when Christ stepped forward to enter the cosmos, then it was that it became meaningful. When the Son of God agreed to the Incarnation, He gave the cosmos its raison d'etre. He became its light. When God said "Let their be light" He said it because the Incar-nate Word stood there in readiness to enter our cosmos.

It was Christ who detonated the Big Bang, who then sup-ported its driving force from the exploding center out to the edge of the expanding ripple of matter and energy. He delineates the edge of space where light ceases to be. "Ego eimi to phos tou kosmou -- I am the light of the cosmos," He could say, aware that where there is light, there is He who gives meaning to the universe by subsum-ing it into His knowledge and appreciation. He joyfully offers it to God as its High Priest. The Father and the Spirit consent with Him to make the cosmos be. They do so only because the Son lives in it as its reason for being.

Christ is also the source of light of our faith. He was the pillar of light Who guided the Israelites through the desert into the Promised Land. He is the Milky Way by which the Hunter-Gatherers aspire to walk into heaven after death.

He is the light in the heart of all believers. He shines their pathway for safe travel into heaven. It is the living pathway within us of the Ten Commandments and of the Gospel message. He makes the pathway come to life within us, illumining our minds and warming our hearts. The living pathway is also that fountain of life which Christ turns on in us. It is a spring of living water welling up to eternal life. Christ is the Alpha who made us and the Omega who conducts us to the mansion prepared for us in heaven.

CONCLUSION

The doctrine about original sin teaches us the basic lesson of the meaning of life: God invited Adam to shape his life into a true image of the Divine Being -- his thoughts, words, deeds, and omissions -- to bring to ample fulfillment the original gift of holiness and justice which he had received from God. Adam's life must be a created image and likeness of his Creator.

But Adam experimented with sin, and tasted its disaster. Christ raised him again to be wiser this time, and to finally succeed.

God likewise invites the descendants of Adam to receive Baptism, to respond to His call to live in holiness and justice. Christ lamented over Jerusalem with tears because of the poor response of its people: "As he drew near and saw the city he wept over it, saying, 'Would that even today you knew the things that make for peace! But now they are hid from your eyes'" (Lk 19:41-42).

Whatever choice humans make during their lives, whether

they do evil and so finally deserve to be ferried by Charon across the Acheron into the place of damnation; or whether they do good finally and so merit to enter into the New Jerusalem to be welcomed by Christ; this Christ is forever the Primate, the Light which makes our cosmos sparkle:

> You are the fairest of the sons of men;
>   grace is poured out upon your lips;
>   therefore God has blessed you forever.
> Gird your sword upon your thigh, O mighty one,
>   In your splendor and your majesty!
>
> In your majesty ride forth victoriously
> for the cause of truth and to defend the right
> (Ps 45:2-4).

Saint Hippolytus celebrates Christ the Pantocrator with a magnificent encomium now featured in the new Catechism:

> Life extends over all beings and fills them with unlimited light; the Orient of orients pervades the universe, and he who was "before the daystar" and before the heavenly bodies, immortal and vast, the Christ, shines over all beings more brightly than the sun. Therefore a day of long, eternal light is ushered in for us who believe in him, a day which is never blotted out: the mystical Passover (see *CCC* 1165).

REFERENCES AND BIBLIOGRAPHY

Alszeghy, Z. and M. Flick, "Il peccato originale in prospettiva evoluzionistica," GREGORIANUM 57 (1966), pp. 201-225.

Amniot, Fr., THE CONCEPTS OF ST. PAUL, trans. by John Dingle, New York, Herder, 1962.

Anchel, Melvin, M.D. "The David Koresh Affair" in SOCIAL JUSTICE REVIEW, May/June 1994.

Anselm of Canterbury, Vol. III, CUR DEUS HOMO (WHY GOD BECAME A MAN), Ed. and Tr. J. Hopkins and H. Richardson, The Edwin Mellen Press, New York, 1976.

Aquinas, Thomas, SUMMA THEOLOGICA, Tr. by Fathers of the English Dominican Province, Benziger Bros., New York, 1948.

ARNOLDUS NOTA, SVD Newsletter.

Ashley, Benedict, O.P. See CATHOLIC WORLD REPORT.

Augustine, Saint, BASIC WRITINGS OF SAINT AUGUSTINE, Vol. I & II, Ed. Whitney J. Oates, Random House, New York, 1948.

- CONFESSIONS, excerpts in THE TREASURY OF CATHOLIC WISDOM, ed. John A. Hardon, S.J., New York, Doubleday, 1987.

- THE LITERAL MEANING OF GENESIS, Vol. I & II, Tr. and annotated by John H. Taylor, S.J., New York, Newman Press, 1982.

Augros, Robert & George Stanciu, THE NEW BIOLOGY, New Science Library Shambhala, Boston & London,1987.

Ballard, P.H., THOUGHT AND LANGUAGE, College Park, Maryland; McGrath, 1970.

Balthasar, Hans Ur von, THE SCANDAL OF THE INCARNATION, passages from Irenaeus AGAINST THE HERESIES; trans. John Saward; Ignatius Press, San Francisco,1990.

BALTIMORE CATECHISM No.2, Tan Books and Publishers, Inc. Rockford, Illinois 61105 USA.

Barnouw, Victor, PHYSICAL ANTHROPOLOGY AND ARCHAEOLOGY, rev. ed. London, England; Georgetown, Ontario, 1975.

Bayer, C., S.J., DE DEO CREANTE ET ELEVANTE, ed. 2, Gregorianum, Rome 1933, pp.420-421.

Berndt, Catherine H. and Ronald M., "Australian Aborigines: Blending Past and Present," in VANISHING PEOPLES OF THE EARTH, Washington, D.C., National Geographic Society, 1968, 114-130.

Bible: Scripture quotations, unless otherwise noted, are from THE REVISED STANDARD VERSION BIBLE, Catholic Edition, copyright 1965 and 1966 by the Division of Christian Education of the National Council of the Churches of Christ in the USA. Used by permission.

- NIB, THE NEW INTERPRETER'S BIBLE, Vol. I, Abington Press, 1994, Nashville, Tenn.

- NIV, NEW INTERNATIONAL VERSION, Zondervan Bible Publishers, Grand Rapids, Michigan, 1984.

Biblioteca De Autores Cristianos, SAC. THEOL. SUMMA, II, Madrid, 1958.

Bird, David, "Evolution: Fact or Faith?" P.O. Box 451, Doncaster Vic 3108, Australia, 1992.

Bliven, Bruce, "The Memory: Remarkable Storage Battery," in OUR HUMAN BODY, pp. 52-56.

Boyer, C., S.J., DE DEO CREANTE ET ELEVANTE, ed. 2, Bregorianum, Rome, 1933, pp. 420-421).

Brain, Robert, THE LAST PRIMITIVE PEOPLES, New York, Crown Pub., 1976.

Brandewie, Ernest, WILHELM SCHMIDT AND THE ORIGIN OF THE IDEA OF GOD, University Press of America, Lanham-New York-London, 1983.

Brinton, D.G. THE LENAPE AND THEIR LEGENDS, Philadelphia, 1885. (Washington: Smithsonian.)

Brooks, Jim, ORIGINS OF LIFE, Lion Publishing Co., Belleville, Michigan, USA, 1985.

Brough-Smythe, THE ABORIGINES OF VICTORIA, Melbourne-London, 1878.

Campbell, Bernard G., Humankind Emerging, Sixth Edition, Harper Collins Publishers, New York, 1992.

Cantley, Msgr. Michael J., "The Biblical Doctrine of Original Sin," PROCEEDINGS, Catholic Theological Society of America, Office of Secretary, Loyola Un. Chicago; Vol. 22, 1967, pp. 133-171.

CATECHISM OF THE CATHOLIC CHURCH, Libreria Editrice Vaticana, United States Catholic Conference, 1994.

CATHOLIC ENCYCLOPEDIA, Ed. Peter Stravinskas, Our Sunday Visitor Press, Huntington IN, 1991.

CATHOLIC WORLD REPORT, monthly journal; ed. office in USA, P.O. Box 1328, Dedham, MA 02027.

COMMUNIO, International Catholic Review, published quarterly, Box 4557, Washington DC 20017-0557 USA.

CONCILIUM TRIDENTINUM, edit. societas Goerresiana.

Connor, James L., S.J., "Original Sin: Contemporary Approaches," THEOLOGICAL STUDIES, 1968, pp. 215-240.

Coulson, Dr. William, "We overcame their traditons, we overecame their faith" in The Latin Mass, Special Edition, 1994.

Crenson, Matt, Associated Press, 16 November, 1996.

CT: CONCILIUM TRIDENTINUM, ed. Societas Goerresiana, Frieburg, Herder, 1965; Vol. I, Vol. V.

Darwin, Charles, 1859/1964. ON THE ORIGIN OF SPE-

CIES. Facsimile ed. Cambridge, Mass.: Harvard University Press.

De Beer, Sir Gavin, HANDBOOK ON EVOLUTION, 3rd ed., London, British Museum of Natural History, 1964.

Deferrari, Roy J., THE SOURCES OF CATHOLIC DOGMA (translation of the 30th ed. of Denzinger), Herder, 1957; now published by Marian House, Powers Lake, N.D. 58773.

Delaney, John, DICTIONARY OF SAINTS, New York, Doubleday, 1980.

Divino Afflante Spiritu, Encyclical Letter of Pope Pius XII on Promotion of Biblical Studies, 30 September 1943.

Dixon, Roland B., "Maidu Myths," BULLETIN OF THE AMERICAN MUSEUM OF NATURAL HISTORY XVII (1902).

DS: Denzinger-Schoenmetzer, ENCHIRIDION SYMBOLORUM, 34th ed., Herder, NY, 1967.

Dubarle, Andre-Marie, O.P., THE BIBLICAL DOCTRINE OF ORIGINAL SIN, trans. by E.M. Stewart; New York, Herder, 1964.

Duffy, Stephen J., "Our hearts of darkness: original sin revisited" in THEOLOGICAL STUDIES 49 (1988) pp. 587-622.

Dulbecco, Renato, THE DESIGN OF LIFE, Yale University

Press, New Haven and London, 1987.

Dupuis, Jacques, S.J., THE CHRISTIAN FAITH, Sixth
Revised and Enlarged Edition, 1996 Theological Publica-
tions in India, published in the United States by Alba
House, N.Y.

Duquoc, Fr. Christian O.P., "New Approaches to Original
Sin" in CROSS CURRENTS Quarterly, Summer 1978, pp.
189-200.

ENCYCLOPEDIA BRITANNICA, 1973 Edition.

Endres, John, O.P. "The Council of Trent and Original Sin"
in PROCEEDINGS, Catholic Theological Society of America, Office of Secretary, Loyola Un. Chicago; Vol. 22,
1967, pp. 70-91.

ETHICS AND MEDICS, monthly publication of The Pope
John Center, Braintree, Massachussetts.

Eusebius, THE HISTORY OF THE CHURCH, trans. by G.A.
Williamson, rev. ed. Penguin Books, London, New York,
1965.

Foster, Elizabeth, THE ABORIGINES FROM PREHISTORY
TO THE PRESENT, Melbourne, Oxford University Press,
1985.

Fowler, Thomas R., SC.D., "Molecular Biology and Evolution: The Crisis and the Challenge" in FAITH AND REA-
SON, Vol. XIX, Fall 1933.

Fox, Stuard Ira, HUMAN PHYSIOLOGY, Wm. Brown Publishers, College Division, Dubuque, Iowa, 1984.

Gannon, Msgr. Timothy J., Ph.D., Prof. Em. Psychology, "Human Sexuality" unpublished manuscript, Loras College, Dubuque, Iowa, 1989, used with permission.

Gill, Dr. Patrick, "Did Man Evolve," summary of lecture, Newman Graduate Education, Bowen St., Chattswood, NSW 2067, Australia, 1990.

Gilder, George, MEN AND MARRIAGE, Pelican Publishing Co., 1101 Monroe Street. Gretna, Louisiana 70053, USA, third printing 1989.

Gini, Corrado, POPULATION, Lectures on the Harris Foundation, 1929, Chicago, University of Chicago Press, 1930.

Grelot, P., "Reflexions sur le probleme du peche originel," NOUVELLE REVEU THEOLOGIQUE 99 (1967) pp.337-375, 449-484.

GS: Gaudium et Spes, Vatican II, Pastoral Constitution of the Church in the Modern World, 7 December 1965; trans. gen. ed. Austin Flannery, O.P. Northport, New York, Castello Press, 1975.

Gusinde, Martin, SVD: see Schmidt, Vol. II.

Hardon, John A., S.J., MODERN CATHOLIC DICTIONARY, Doubleday, NY, 1980.

HARPER'S BIBLICAL COMMENTARY, General Editor James L. Mays, Harper and Row, San Francisco, 1988.

HARPER'S BIBLE DICTIONARY, General Editor Paul J. Achtemeier, San Francisco, 1985.

Harrington,, M.R., RELIGION AND CEREMONIES OF THE LENAPE, INDIAN NOTES AND MONOGRAPHS, New York, Heye Foundation, 1921.

Henrichi, Peter, "The Spiritual Dimension and its Form of Reason" in Communio, Winter 1993, pp. 638-651.

Herve, J.M., MANUALE THEOLOGICAE DOGMATICAE, 4 Vol   umes; Vol. II, Ed. 17, Newman Bookshop, Westminster,   MD., 1946.

Hildebrand, Dietrich Von, TROJAN HORSE IN THE CITY OF GOD, Sophia Institute Press, Box 5284, Manchester, New Hampshire 03108 USA, 1993.

HLI Reports, Human Life International monthly, Paul Marx, OSB, editor, 7845-E Airpark Road, Gaithersburg MD, USA. Now at 4 Family Life, Front Royal, Virginia 22630. (See also Marx.)

Holboeck, Ferdinand, CREDIMUS, Pustet, Salzburg-Muenchen, 1970.

HPR: HOMILETIC AND PASTORAL REVIEW (monthly).

Hughes, Philip, A HISTORY OF THE CHURCH, Vol. II, Sheed and Ward, New York, 1947.

- THE CHURCH IN CRISIS, A History of the General Councils, 325-1870, Image Books, Doubleday, New York, 1961.

Hulsbosch, A, OSA, GOD IN CREATION AND EVOLUTION, trans. by M. Versfeld, Sheed and Ward, New York, 1965.

Humani Generis, Encyclical Letter of Pope Pius XII, 1950.

INSIDE THE VATICAN, monthly journal, Viale delle Mura Aurelie 7c, Rome 00165, Italy.

IRENAEUS, St. ADVERSUS HAERESES, 5 books, PG 7.

- PROOF OF THE APOSTOLIC PREACHING, Trans. by Joseph P. Smith, S.J., Ancient Christian Writers, ed. by Quasten and Plumpe, No. 16; the Newman Press, Westminster, Maryland, 1952.

Jaki, Fr. Stanley, Interview in OUR SUNDAY VISITOR, conducted by Bill Dodds, 14 February 1993.

JAPAN MISSION JOURNAL, THE, quarterly, Oriens Institute for Religious Research, 28-5 Matsubara 2 chome, Setagaya-ku, Tokyo 156.

Jedin, M., A HISTORY OF THE COUNCIL OF TRENT, Vol.1 & 2, (German original) Herder, Freiburg, 1957; Engl. Trans. Dom E. Graf, Nelson and Sons, New York, 1961.

Jennings, Jesse D., "Across an Arctic Bridge," in THE WORLD OF THE AMERICAN INDIAN, Washington D.C.,

National Geographic Society, 1979.

Johanson, Donald C., and Maitland A. Edey, LUCY, THE BEGINNINGS OF HUMANKIND, New York, Simon and Schuster, 1981.

John Paul II, see OSSERVATORE ROMANO, Weekly Edition in English, on date following the Wednesday Catechesis, for English versions of cited address.

- ORIGINAL UNITY OF MAN AND WOMAN, Catechesis on the Book of Genesis, Daughters of St. Paul, Boston, 1981.

- Familiaris Consortio, Feast of Christ the King, 1981.

- Veritatis Splendor, October 5, 1993, (August 6, 1993).

- Message to the Pontifical Academy of Sciences, 22 October 1996.

- Message to the Pontifical Academy of Sciences, 29 November 1996.

Jurgens, William A., THE FAITH OF THE EARLY FATHERS, The Liturgical Press, Collegeville MN, 1970.

Keane, G.J., CREATION REDISCOVERED, Credis Pty Ltd, Australia, 1991.

Kelly, Petra, "Growing up Green" New Age Journal, November-December 1987, p. 73, quoted by Aiden Nichols OP in "The New Age Movement" THE JAPAN MISSION

JOURNAL, Spring 1994, p. 83.

Kenny, J.P., "Concupiscence" in THE NEW CATHOLIC ENCYCLOPEDIIA.

Kenyatta, Jomo, FACING MOUNT KENYA, edited by J. Kariuki; Heinemann Kenya Ltd., Nairobi, reprinted 1991.

Koszarek, Sister Clare, S.S.J., THE CATECHESIS OF ORIG-INAL SIN, St. John's University Press, Collegeville MN, 1969.

Kroeber, A.L., "Wishosk Myths," JOURNAL OF AMERICAN FOLKLORE XVIII, (April-June 1905). Kraus Reprint Co., Millwood, N.Y. 1979.

Kselman, Fr. John, SS, "Genesis" in HARPER'S BIBLICAL COMMENTARY, Harper and Row, San Francisco, 1988, p. 88.

Lawler, Robert, VOICES OF THE FIRST DAY, Inner Traditions International, Ltd. One Park Street, Rochester, Vermont, 1991.

Leakey, Richard E., ONE LIFE, AN AUTOBIOGRAPHY, Salem, New Hampshire, Salem House, 1986.

- "Homo Erectus Unearthed," in NATIONAL GEOGRAPHIC 168, (November 1985, 624-630.

Lejeune, Jerome, M.D., "Is there a Natural Morality?" in LINACRE QUARTERLY, February, 1989.

- "Testimony in the Blount County Tennessee Court," August 10, 1989; Center for Law & Religious Freedom, 4208 Evergreen Lane, Suite 222, Annandale, Virginia 22003, USA.

Lennenberg, Eric E., BIOLOGICAL FOUNDATIONS FOR LANGUAGE, with appendices by Noam Chomsky and Otto Marx. New York: John Wiley and Sons, 1967.

Lewin, Roger, IN THE AGE OF MANKIND, Smithsonian Books, Washington DC, 1988.

LG: Lumen Gentium, Vatican II, Dogmatic Constitution on the Church, 21 November 11964. See GS above.

Lieberman, Philip, THE BIOLOGY AND EVOLUTION OF LANGUAGE, Harvard University Press, Cambridge, MA, 1984.

- "On the Evolution of Human Syntactic Ability ...," JOURNAL OF HUMAN EVOLUTION 14, (1985), 657-68.

- THE EVOLUTION OF UNIQUELY HUMAN SPEECH, THOUGHT AND HUMAN SELFLESS BEHAVIOR, Harvard University Press, 1991.

MacLean, Paul D., A TRIUNE CONCEPT OF THE BRAIN, Toronto University Press, 1973.

Margerie, Fr. Bertrand de, S.J., THE EXEGESIS OF THE FATHERS OF THE CHURCH: VOL. III - ST. AUGUSTINE, St. Bede's Publications, P.O. Box 545, St. Petersham, Mass. 01366 USA. See review in HOMILETIC AND PAS-

TORAL REVIEW, May 1994, p. 78.

Martin, Francis, "Male and female he created them: A summary of the teaching of Genesis chapter one," in COMMUNIO, International Catholic Review, published quarterly, Box 4557, Washington DC 20017-0557 USA, Summer 1993, pp. 240-265.

Marx, Paul, OSB, "A Catholic Analysis of Programs on Sex Ed," a series of six pamphlets produced by theologians and concerned parents and edited by himself, 1991-1993, Human Life International, 4 Family Life, Front Royal Virginia 22630.

Masi, Roberto, "Theology of Original Sin" in OSSERVATO-RE ROMANO, Weekly ed. in English, 17 April 1969.

Massarelli, Angelini, CONCILII TRIDENTINI DIARIORUM; II, Ed. S. Merkle, Herder, Friburg, 1965.

Migne, J.P., PATROLOGIAE CURSUS COMPLETUS, PG Vol. VII, CONTRA HAERESES; reprint by Brepols, Turn-hout, Belgium, 1988. Latin quotations are from here; English translations, unless indicated otherwise, are by the author.

Minns, Denis, OP, IRENAEUS, Georgetown University Press, Washington DC, 20007, 1994.

Moraczewski, Albert S., O.P., "Genes and Pandora's Box" in ETHICS AND MEDICS (see list), March 1993.

Murphy, John L., GENERAL COUNCILS OF THE CHURCH,

Bruce, Milwaukee, 1960.

NATIONAL GEOGRAPHIC, Monthly, National Geographic Society, Washington, D.C.

Nemesszeghy, S.J. and John Russell, S.J., THEOLOGY OF EVOLUTION, Clergy Book Service, Butler, WI 1972.

NEW CATHOLIC ENCYCLOPEDIA, THE, New York: McGraw Hill, 1967 (edited by the staff of the Catholic University of America).

NIB, THE NEW INTERPRETER'S BIBLE, Vol. I, Abington Press, Nashville, 1994.

Nichols, Aidan, OP, "The New Age Movement" in THE JAPAN MISSION JOURNAL, Spring 1994, pp. 78-86.

Noldin, Godefridus, S.J., Schmidt S.J. Heinzel, S.J., SUMMA THEOLOGIAE MORALIS, 3 Vol., Oenipotente, Rauch, ;ed. XXXI, 1956.

O'Mahony, Fr. Thomas, "The Suicide of the Missions," in CHRISTIAN ORDER, March 1992, pp. 175-179).

OSSERVATORE ROMANO, Weekly Edition in English, Vatican Polyglot Press.

Ott, Dr. Ludwig, FUNDAMENTAL OF CATHOLIC DOGMA, Trans. by Lunch, Ed. by Bastible, Tan Publishers, Rockford IL, 1974.

OUR HUMAN BODY, Pegasus Books, Reader's Digest

Association, 1968.

OUR SUNDAY VISITOR, National Catholic Weekly, Huting-
ton, IN, USA.

Padovano, Anthony T., "Original Sin and Christian Anthropology," Corpus Books, Washington & Cleveland, 1969.

Pancheri, Francis X., O.F.M. THE UNIVERSAL PRIMACY
OF CHRIST, Tr. J. Carol, O.F.M., Christendom Publications, Front Royal VA, 1984.

PATROLOGY, Vol. III, The Christian Classics, Westminster
MD, 1992.

PATROLOGY, Vol. IV, ed. by Angelo Di Berardino, trans.
by Rev. Placid Solari, O.S.B., Christian Classics, Westminster MD, 1986.

Peacock, Roy E., A BRIEF HISTORY OF ETERNITY, Cross-
way Books, Wheaton, Illinois, 1990.

Pfeiffer, John, THE EMERGENCE OF MAN, New York,
Harper and Row, 1969.

- "Introducing the Brain" in OUR HUMAN BODY, pp. 46-
51.

Pius XII, Pope, Christmas Message of 1957; see Vol II,
THE MAJOR ADDRESSES OF POPE PIUS XII, ed. by Vin-
cent A. Yzermans, North Central Publishing Co., St. Paul,
Minnesota, USA, 1961.

230   REFERENCES

- Encyclical Letter HUMANI GENERIS, 1950.

POPE SPEAKS, THE, Quarterly, Our Sunday Visitor Press, Vol. 29, No. 1, Huntington IN, 1984.

Porier, Frank, William A. Stini, Kahy B. Wreden, IN SEARCH OF OURSELVES, An Introduction to Physical Anthropolgy, Prentice Hall, Englewood Cliffs, New Jersey, Fourth edition, 1990.

Powers, Stephen, "Tribes of California," BULLETIN OF AMERICAN ETHNOLOGY, Washington, Smithsonian, 1877.

Presland, Gary, THE LAND OF THE KULIN, Fitzroy, Victoria, Australia, McPhee Gribble/Penguin Books, 1985.

Quasten, Johannes, PATROLOGY, Vol. I & II, The Newman Press, Westminster MD 1951.

Rahner, Karl, S.J., ON THE THEOLOGY OF DEATH; Quaes. Disp. No. 2, Tr. by Henkey, New York, Herder, 2nd English ed.,1967.

- HOMINIZATION, Quaes. Disp. No. 13; Tr. by W.J. O'Hara, New York, Herder, 1965.

Ramsey, Boniface, BEGINNING TO READ THE FATHERS, Paulist Press, Mahwah, New York, 1985.

Ratcliff, J.D. and others, "Our Busy Bones" in OUR HUMAN BODY, see list, pp. 113-118).

Renckens, H. S.J., ISRAEL'S CONCEPT OF THE BEGIN-
NING, New York, Herder, 1964.

Ricoeur, P., "Original Sin: A Study in Meaning," in THE
CONFLICT OF INTERPRETATIONS: ESSAYS IN HERME-
NEUTICS, ed. D. Ihde (Evanston, Illinois, USA: North-
western University, 1974) 272-273).

Roetzer, Josef, M.D., "Medical Anthropology and Respon-
sible Procreation" in "Humanae Vitae 20 Anni Dopo,"
Pontifical Institute of John Paul II, Lateran University,
Rome, 1989.

Rooney, David, "The First Religion of Mankind," in FAITH
AND REASON, monthly, Fall 1993.

Rose, J.J. see Schmidt below.

Saward: See Balthasar above.

Schaefer, Vernon J., Father, "Classroom sex education: in
HPR, March 1995.

Scheeben, Matthias Joseph, THE MYSTERIES OF CHRIS-
TIANITY, Trans. by Vollert, S.J., St. Louis MO, Herder,
1958.

SCHEMATA CONSTITUTIONUM ET DECRETORUM, de
quibus discetabitur in Concillii sessionibus, Series Prima,
1962.

Schmaus, Michael, DOGMA, Vol. II, God and Creation,
Christian Classics, Westminster, MD, 1984.

- MAN AND SIN, The Un. of Notre Dame Press, Notre Dame IN, 1965.

Schmidt, Wilhelm, SVD, DER URSPRUNG DER GOTTES IDEE, 12 volumes, Frieburg, Switzerland, Anthropos Institute, 1926-1955.

- HANDBUCH DER VERGLEICHENDEN RELIGIONSGE-SHICHTE, Muenster in Westphalen, 1930. Trans. by J.J. Rose, London: Methuen and Co., 1931.

Schoonenberg, Piet, S.J., "Some Remarks on the Present Discussion of Original Sin," Lecture at Sturzo Hall, Rome, 23 November 1967; IDO-C Bulletin.

- MAN AND SIN, Notre Dame Press, 1965.

Seguin, Michael, "The biblical foundations of the thought of John Paul II on human sexuality," in COMMUNIO, September 1993, pp. 266-289.

Smith, Joseph, S.J. ST. IRENAEUS, PROOF OF THE AP-OSTOLIC PREACHING, No. 16 of Ancient Christian Writings; Newman Press, Westminster, Maryland, 1951.

SOCIAL JUSTICE REVIEW, bi-monthly, Catholic Central Union, St. Louis, Missouri, USA.

Speck, Frank Gouldsmith, A STUDY OF THE DELAWARE INDIAN BIGHOUSE CEREMONY, University of Pennsylvania, Pennsylvania Historical Commission, Harrisburg, 1931.

Strecker, Edward A., et al., DISCOVERING OURSELVES: New York: Macmillan, 1958.

Strong, John, EXHAUSTIVE CONCORDANCE OF THE BIBLE, With Dictionaries of the Hebrew and Greek Words of the Original, Hendrickson Publisheers, Peabody, Massachussetts (no date of publication given.

Tennant, F.R., THE SOURCES OF THE DOCTRINES OF THE FALL AND ORIGINAL SIN, Schocken Books, New York, 1968. First published in 1903.

Thiesen, A. and P. Byrne, "Romans" in A NEW CATHOLIC COMMENTARY ON HOLY SCRIPTURE, London, Nelson, 1969).

Tixeront, J, A HISTORY OF DOGMAS, 3 Vol., St. Louis, Herder, 1914.

TPS, THE POPE SPEAKS, Quarterly, Our Sunday Visitor Press, Huntington, IN, USA.

Vawter, Fr. Bruce, C.M., "Genesis" in A NEW CATHOLIC COMMENTARY ON HOLY SCRIPTURE, Thomas Nelson and sons, revised 1969, pp. 166-206).

Weaver, Kenneth, "The Search for our Ancestors," NATIONAL GEOGRAPHIC, 168 (November 1985).

Weiss, Mark L., and Alane E. Mann, HUMAN BIOLOGY AND BEHAVIOR - AN ANTHROPOLOGICAL PERSPECTIVE, 4th ed. Boston-Toronto: Little, Brown and Company, 1985.

Whitcomb, John C. Jnr., THE WORLD THAT PERISHED, Evangelical Press, London, 1974.

Willis, John R., S.J. THE TEACHING OF THE CHURCH FATHERS, New York, Herder, 1966.

Wylie, Evan McLeod, "All about Your Throat," in OUR HUMAN BODY, Reader's Digest, Pegasus Books,1968, pp. 96-100.

Young, John, "Original Sin: A controverted doctrine" in HOMILETIC AND PASTORAL REVIEW, December 1988, pp.9-16.

Zimmerman, Anthony, SVD, ORIGINAL SIN: WHERE DOC-TRINE MEETS FAITH, New York, Vantage Press, 506 W. 34th St., 1990.

- THE RELIGION OF ADAM AND EVE, New York, Vantage Press, 506 W. 34th St., 1991.

- CATHOLIC VIEWPOINT ON OVERPOPULATION, Catholic Viewpoint Series, John J. Delaney, editor, New York, Doubleday, 1961.

- NATURAL FAMILY PLANNING, Nature's Way - God's Way, Milwaukee, De Rance, 1980.

INDEX

ABOUT THE AUTHOR

Father Anthony Zimmerman, STD, came to Japan as a Catholic missionary fifty years ago. He is a retired Professor of Moral Theology at Nanzan University, Nagoya, and frequently contributes to journals and publications on religious subjects and pro-life issues.

He is a member of the Fellowship of Catholic Scholars, of the Society of Catholic Social Scientists, the International Union for the Scientific Study of Population, and other academic groups.

Anthony Zimmerman, STD
Hitoshi Building #602
Ueda 3, 1205, Tempaku-ku
Nagoya 468-0051, JAPAN

nb5a-zmmr@Asahi-net.or.jp